MW00487546

NELSON RIDDLE
Music With a Heartbeat

An Authorised Biography

Geoffrey Littlefield

with

Christopher Riddle

Grosvenor House
Publishing Limited

All rights reserved
Copyright © Geoffrey Littlefield, 2021

The right of Geoffrey Littlefield to be identified as the author of this
work has been asserted in accordance with Section 78
of the Copyright, Designs and Patents Act 1988

The book cover is copyright to Geoffrey Littlefield
Cover design by Ray Leaning

This book is published by
Grosvenor House Publishing Ltd
Link House
140 The Broadway, Tolworth, Surrey, KT6 7HT.
www.grosvenorhousepublishing.co.uk

This book is sold subject to the conditions that it shall not, by way of
trade or otherwise, be lent, resold, hired out or otherwise circulated
without the author's or publisher's prior consent in any form of binding or
cover other than that in which it is published and
without a similar condition including this condition being imposed
on the subsequent purchaser.

A CIP record for this book
is available from the British Library

ISBN 978-1-83975-440-1

I dedicate this book to my wife Hilary, my son Gary, my daughter Bonnie, son-in-law Kim, and my two amazing granddaughters Jacqueline and Abbeygale.

Special Thanks

Christopher Riddle

CONTENTS

Frank Sinatra and Nelson Riddle confer about the music for
For Only The Lonely. Photography courtesy of Pete Christlieb.

INTRODUCTION

NELSON RIDDLE was quite possibly the greatest; one of most successful and prolific composers and arrangers in the history of American popular music. Over the course of his long and distinguished career, he was also a conductor, a trombonist, and an occasional hitmaker in his own right. He worked with many of the biggest global stars of his day - Dean Martin, Peggy Lee, Judy Garland and many more. And in a time of segregation and deep racial tensions in the US, he not only worked with leading black artists such as Nat King Cole and Ella Fitzgerald but formed close personal friendships with them too. But above all of this, it was Nelson's immortal work with FRANK SINATRA at Capitol Records, that cemented his enduring legacy.

We delve deep into an extraordinary musical legacy that saw Riddle win one of the first Grammy's, an Oscar (after five nominations) for *The Great Gatsby* and spawned countless hit singles and albums.

Through family photograph albums of recording sessions, live performances and interviews with those who knew him well, my book explores the musical genius behind some of the greatest popular tunes of the 20th Century. My own knowledge and expertise in that field has been greatly enhanced by this journey of discovery.

Like so many creative souls, Riddle was a complex and troubled figure; his marriage to Doreen, with whom he had seven children, was rocky to say the least.

The maestro led a complicated and troubled personal life - perhaps never really finding the kind of peace or success in his private life that he enjoyed in his professional one. His marriage was constantly under threat by his numerous affairs.

When Sinatra chose to have his own 'professional sleeping around' with other arrangers in the late 1950s, Riddle began another fruitful collaboration, recording with Ella Fitzgerald. Their work together included three of her landmark "songbook" albums, devoted to George and Ira Gershwin, Jerome Kern and Johnny Mercer.

Success in films and television followed too. In 1966, Riddle was hired to write music for the TV series, *Batman*. More TV themes followed - *Route 66, The Untouchables*, and *Tarzan* - and acclaimed movies including *Ocean's Eleven* and Kubrick's *Lolita*. And in 1974, after five nominations, Riddle won the Academy Award for his score to *The Great Gatsby*.

Riddle never retired; he continued to work in film and television and toured with the Nelson Riddle Orchestra. But the traditional genre in which he specialised had gone out of style, and it was a surprise when he was approached in 1982 by Linda Ronstadt, who wanted to record an album of standards. Riddle was hesitant. He'd been approached by pop singers in the past and had turned them down when all they wanted was a single song, which he thought would be jarring and out of place in the middle of a modern rock album. Ronstadt agreed to do a full album, and Riddle's daughter Rosemary, a Ronstadt fan, told him, "Don't worry, Dad.

Her checks won't bounce." So, Riddle signed on for what became a three-album project. The albums, *What's New? Lush Life* and *For Sentimental Reasons* were hugely successful the first two going platinum, reviving interest in Riddle's career among a new generation of fans.

Sinatra and Riddle in Capitol Records recording session.
Photograph courtesy of Rosemary Acerra's personal collection.

1. I'VE GOT YOU UNDER MY SKIN

And each time that I do,
just the thought of you

"Capitol Records wanted to give Frank a new set of clothes. I guess I was his tailor." Nelson Riddle

It was a momentous period. Frank Sinatra off the back of two years of unparalleled success as an actor and new-born singer of swing, arrived at studio A to record four songs with Nelson Riddle for a concept album[1] called *Songs For Swingin' Lovers.*

Sinatra liked to record at night as he felt his vocal pipes were much looser. It was Monday the 9th of January 1956, KHJ Radio Studios on Melrose Avenue in Los Angeles, USA. As was the norm, he was accompanied by an entourage of various people. This included the great and the not-so-good of Hollywood, a number of whom would sit through the recording sessions.

Musicians commented that the studio should have charged admission as the studio was always full to the rafters. Consequently, Capitol Records had taken a calculated risk, as applause would ring out, and a number of takes had to be aborted.

---

[1] a concept album is one where the tracks are tied together by one theme both lyrically and musically.

The group that congregated that night in Studio A consisted of some of the finest classical string players and jazz instrumentalists around. Sinatra demanded no less. There was Eleanor and Felix Slatkin, a cellist and Sinatra's concertmaster respectively. On bass trombone was George Roberts together with minimalist trumpeter Harry "Sweets" Edison. The orchestra also included valve trombonist Juan Tizol (who composed the song "Caravan"), alto saxophonist Harry Klee who doubled on flute, and pianist Bill Miller — then there was the trombonist Milt Bernhart.

The planning of this album took place some six months earlier when Sinatra and Nelson had a business lunch at the Villa Capri restaurant in Hollywood. Sinatra delivered precise details to Nelson about what he wanted. Nelson, writing fast as always, took copious notes to the point of ending with a splitting headache. Sinatra had asked Nelson for a background of "sustained strings". Nelson could hear the band playing in his head and visualise the result. He used the piano keys to formulate his ideas.

"Frank wanted a crescendo, then I come down so he could finish it off. There weren't too many pre-recording discussions other than that. I know he was incredibly pleased when he heard the final tape and especially over the next day or so, as he was playing it back constantly. It became regarded as a cornerstone recording for the two of us."

Nelson was impressed by Ravel's "Bolero" and its dynamic and the crescendo where it builds and builds throughout the tune. When he was fifteen years old he attended a concert at New York's Carnegie Hall and heard Serge Koussevitsky with the Boston Symphony perform "Bolero". Such a calculated crescendo as in

"Bolero" impressed Nelson so much he drew on that experience in his future works, the most iconic example of effective use of crescendi is in "I've Got You Under My Skin"—requested by Sinatra, delivered by Riddle. It helped immortalise the song.

Nelson added the bass trombone played by George Roberts and a muted trumpet played by "Sweets" Edison, played in his usual understated fashion.

Nelson would later say, "I don't think Frank was aware of how I was going to achieve a long crescendo." Sinatra was also looking for an instrumental interlude, so he could come in and finish the song. Nelson achieved his objective but not without drawing on his study of the classical composers like Ravel and Debussy. He also sought advice from a trusted lieutenant in George Roberts who referred him to a piece Stan Kenton had written. George suggested he may like to borrow a little from that.

Christopher Riddle: "Dad brought Harry Edison over from the Count Basie Band. He was a great trumpeter but was used to playing by ear, so my father paid for him to read music, as he wanted him to play lots of trumpet solos. For Harry to sit in the section, he had to learn to read some."

All the basic ingredients to produce the album were in place. The first two recording sessions went well, with the second session finishing in the early hours of Wednesday morning, the 11th January. In the meantime, Alan Livingston, vice-president at Capitol Records, had decided to capitalise further on the undoubted success of the album, which lay ahead. He wanted three tunes added. This did not go down well with Sinatra, who was livid at this request as he had planned to spend the next day or so at his Palm Springs home to recover some energy.

Livingston's instruction meant an extra recording session would now take place on Thursday 12th January. Sinatra got right on it and phoned Nelson at home, waking him up in the process. He gave Nelson three more songs which needed to be arranged "immediately".

Nelson got out of bed and got to work. He knew Sinatra would not be in a good mood doing an extra, unplanned recording session. This added pressure seemed to supercharge Nelson.

Christopher Riddle: "My father thrived on working with his back to the wall and invariably produced his best when working under pressure."

By Thursday morning, Nelson had arranged two of the songs. Writing music arrangements is a complex and labour-intensive task, but Nelson always worked fast. The two songs were "It Happened in Monterrey" and "Swinging Down the Lane". He immediately got these two arrangements to the copyist, Vern Yocum. But even Nelson needed sleep, so he grabbed a couple of hours, then started writing again early that afternoon. The remaining song to be arranged was the Cole Porter ballad "I've Got You Under My Skin".

Having worked furiously during the whole afternoon without respite, Nelson set off with his wife, Doreen, at the wheel of their Ford Country Squire station wagon, and early that night, they drove to the studios. Nelson sat on the back seat, torch in hand, writing. Nelson used a leaf from a dining room table as a laptop desk in the back of the car.

When they arrived at the studios, Sinatra had finished recording a song which was to be a future single release, unrelated to the album. In the meantime, Nelson gave the remaining arrangement to the copyist.

Sinatra was christened one-take Charlie when acting in movies, but in the recording studio, he might do four or five takes before getting the song absolutely to his liking. "Skin" was the final recording, and the number of takes exceeded the average. Some said they were tinkering around with instrument microphone placements, getting Milt Bernhart to stand on a box to achieve the right sound from his trombone, as they needed more brass.

George Roberts on bass trombone and the strings lift the long crescendo higher and higher and higher until they can go no further. Milt Bernhart, drawing on reserves he didn't know he possessed, goes wild on his slide trombone, simply blowing his lungs out. Sinatra's powerful final chorus, driving the song home, is as strong in its own right as Bernhart's now historic solo. Bernhart had been out on his feet after five takes, but the session went on take after take, not all full takes, but someone had counted over twenty by the time Sinatra gave the thumbs up.

At the end of the session, the weary band members stood up and applauded Nelson Riddle, appreciative of the little time he had been given to do the "Skin" arrangement. They recognised something special had been achieved.

Nelson, asked in a later interview whether he was feeling elated after completing the marathon session, would say, "I was probably thinking that I was relieved to have completed the arrangement in time." Nelson wasn't physically afraid of Sinatra, but he found his sudden mood changes quite intimidating, saying, "Frank can change so fast."

He had learned this lesson painfully on an aborted early session in his collaboration with Frank. Part way into a take of "Wrap Your Troubles in Dreams", Sinatra stopped the band and beckoned Nelson into the recording booth, explaining heatedly to his ambitious young arranger (Nelson was five and a half years Frank's junior) that he was crowding the singer out, having simply written too many notes, beautiful as the notes might have been. Nelson never made the same mistake again.

It turned out to be a pivotal moment. Sinatra, capable of firing associates on a whim, might have fired Nelson there and then. However, Sinatra was musically aware enough to realize that Nelson was taking him in new and exciting directions.

Quincy Jones recalled, "Nelson was smart because he put the electricity up above Frank and gave Frank the room downstairs for his voice to shine, rather than building lush parts which were in the same register as his voice."

Nelson re-affirmed that once, saying, "In working out arrangements for Frank, I suppose I stuck to two main rules. First, find the peak of the song and build the whole arrangement to that peak, pacing it as he paces himself vocally. Second, when he's moving, get the hell out of the way.... After all, what arranger in the world would try to fight against Sinatra's voice? Give the singer room to breathe. When the singer rests, then there's a chance to write a fill that might be heard." Nelson's worst fears were unfounded in this case as the session which ran into the early hours of Friday the 13th produced "I've Got You Under My Skin", one of the masterpieces in American popular music.

When Sinatra sings against Nelson Riddle strings
Then takes a vacation

"Hard Nose the Highway" Van Morrison

When Frank Sinatra first heard the finished cut for "Skin", he played it over and over, almost twenty-four hours a day. It became synonymous with the Sinatra and Riddle combination and was an integral tune in the smash hit album, widely regarded as Sinatra's finest work.

"Skin" was to elevate the Sinatra/Riddle collaboration to new dizzy heights, with both artists being at the top of their game. In fact, the song written in 1936 by composer Cole Porter as a ballad, was sung by Sinatra in its original form as far back as 1946, some ten years earlier to that night, when the song became immortalised. It is inconceivable today to hear the song as a straight ballad. Nelson Riddle's arrangement had changed the components of the song, aside, of course, from the lyrics which remain the same. In its current form, it should now perhaps be considered to be a Porter/Riddle composition. That frenetic night at KHJ catapulted Nelson Riddle into the higher echelons of American music hierarchy.

Radio personality Jonathan Schwartz of WNEW later remarked, "There are four major influences on American popular music. They are Billy Holiday, Louis Armstrong, Frank Sinatra and Nelson Riddle."

2. LAST NIGHT WHEN WE WERE YOUNG

Last night when we were young
Love was a star

Nelson Smock Riddle II was born on the 1st of June 1921, in Hackensack, New Jersey, USA. His mother, Albertine, was of French Alsace descent, and his father, Nelson Riddle, was of English-Irish-Dutch parentage. The year 1921 was a ground-breaking year. The full-length silent comedy film *The Kid* was written, produced, directed and starred Charlie Chaplin (in his Tramp character). Communist parties were formed that year in Italy, China, and Czechoslovakia.

Nelson's infant years were spent in the roaring twenties, characterised by high employment, and rising living standards. The era of Art Deco was evident in the style of design and architecture. October 1929, however, brought a decade of widespread prosperity to a juddering halt with the Great Depression taking hold.

In those days, the federal government wouldn't print more money, or to use a more modern phrase, apply quantitative easing. Those that were in work paid for their products or services with food. Bartering was also common.

Despite experiencing financial hardships, Nelson was encouraged by his mother and father to study music. His mother loved the classical composers such as Debussy and Ravel and encouraged young Nelson to listen to that genre of music. His father, Nelson Snr, was a commercial artist and was an accomplished amateur musician; he played the trombone. Nelson started his own musical journey by taking piano lessons when he was eight years old. He was a dedicated student, but he decided he had no talent for the piano, preferring to play the trombone which was to become his instrument. He was tutored by a local professor, but his study time was brought to an abrupt halt, as his father was unable to keep up the payments of a dollar a session.

During his junior high school days, his aunt bought Nelson a wind-up gramophone player where he listened to the records which came as part of the gift. He particularly liked the piece by Debussy titled "Reflections on the Water", constantly playing it to the point that the cactus needles were totally blunted in the process. It was listening to composers such as Debussy, Ravel and Walton that encouraged him to plan a career as a musician. He loved the deftness of the impressionists.

Nelson's son Christopher: "When my father was around 15/16 years old, he heard this kid's band rehearsing, and he knocked on the door. Dad was standing there with his trombone and asked if he could play in the band. The reply was, 'We've already got eight people, so we are splitting the check eight ways, and we already have a trombone player.' However, my dad started writing charts for the band. The leader of the band was Eddie Briggs, and the band was the Briggadeers. Eddie used to work at Bell Laboratories where they used to make transistor radios."

In his last year at high school, Nelson persuaded his parents to let him stay in Rumson, New Jersey, a small village where they had rented several rooms each summer. His mother went with him, and his father came down from his studio at weekends.

The rooms at Rumson had no electricity, only gas; the walls being dimly lit by the light provided by gas filaments. Despite that, Nelson continued his music study, gathering as much information as he could. There was no radio available to him at that time, and he had to wait until his father returned from his commercial studio at weekends, when he was able to listen to various kinds of music using his dad's car radio. On many occasions, this resulted in a flat car battery with Nelson Snr. having to crank the engine to get to work the following morning!

It was during a previous stay in Rumson that Nelson met Bill Finegan, whose family had lived in the area for many years.

Christopher Riddle: "Bill Finegan persuaded my grandparents to move there as Dad would then be eligible to attend Rumson High School for his final (senior) year. The reason being that Rumson had a very highly regarded music department. Bill thought this would be of immense help in my father's musical education. Some years back, I attended a ceremony there because my father had been inducted into their Hall of Fame."

Finegan had studied at the famous Paris conservatory which was founded in 1795. He saw something in Nelson; he recognised his special talent and became his mentor. The first assignment Bill gave the young Nelson was to write a chorus of "Swanee River" for saxophones. However, his study with Bill Finegan was brought to a shuddering halt as Bill was required to go on the road with the Glenn Miller Orchestra.

"Half Nelson" – Aged 8yrs with first trombone. Photograph courtesy of Rosemary Acerra's personal collection.

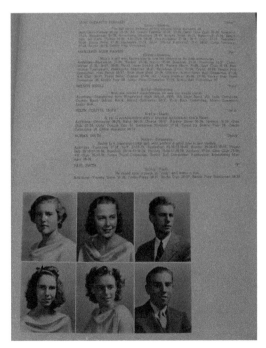

"With his learned dissertations he sets our heads awhirl." Rumson High School yearbook 1939. Photograph courtesy of Christopher Riddle's personal collection.

Nevertheless, Finegan got Nelson on the Charlie Spivak Band, then later on the Merchant Marine Band in 1943, where he was able to avoid the draft. When Nelson got out a year later, Finegan got him on the Tommy Dorsey Band as third arranger. Nelson had idolised Bill Finegan, describing him as one of the front runners of fine arranging. Later on, he was less complimentary about the Sauter-Finegan Orchestra which he considered less than commercial, more cerebral, and for all its beautiful music was lacking in fire, drive and emotion. He felt that it was reflective of the two men's personalities which were rather studious and introspective. He acknowledged, however, that his early arrangements bore the hallmark of Bill Finegan.

Christopher Riddle: "Dad hadn't written anything for strings because the Spivak Band didn't have any. He learned to write for strings in the Merchant Marines at Sheepshead Bay, Brooklyn, New York. A year later, he went to Chicago to join Tommy Dorsey and started to write arrangements for strings. Tommy had to take him aside, however, and told him beautiful as his string arrangements were, he needed to stop writing for them. Tommy said after all, at the end of the day, they're only a tax dodge! Tommy was a wonderful musician, a marvellous trombone player. He could just pick up his trombone then 'spit through it' then go right into sentimental. He was a remarkable musician and a real inspiration for my father."

Dorsey was known as a ruthless and hard taskmaster, yet he nurtured the young arranger. Nelson was initially taken aback when Dorsey had made that comment but it did him a big favour as he went back to his room, and he dreamt up a way to write his arrangements playable with or without strings. He broke two lines for the woodwinds, support for the strings because the strings have the melody. If there are no strings, you play the second line. It was brilliant.

Later on is his career, after Dorsey had passed, Nelson commented, "Every note I write I learned from that man upstairs. People rave over my arranging today, and I just think to myself, God bless Tommy Dorsey. If it hadn't been for him, I never could have done it."

Although Nelson was not with the Dorsey Band at the same time as Frank Sinatra, there was some career parallel. Sinatra would study the exceptional trombone playing by Dorsey, especially his breathing technique, which Sinatra wanted to adapt for his vocalising.

Sinatra was to say, "My greatest teacher was not a vocal coach, not the work of other singers, but the way Tommy Dorsey breathed and phrased on the trombone."

After Dorsey, the army finally caught up with Nelson, and he spent a "fun-packed" fifteen months at Fort Dix primarily as a foot soldier. Then on the 10th October 1945, Nelson married a proud Catholic in Doreen Moran, with whom he would have seven children. As soon as it was announced that the war was over, Nelson was transferred to an army band whilst some eight hundred fellow draftees were assigned overseas. He was able to play in the band there until his honourable discharge in 1946.

Nelson's daughter Rosemary Acerra takes up the story: "Dad was very dedicated to his music. We as a family moved from the east coast to the west coast as in Los Angeles. Dad started working in radio in 1947 and was due to sign with Bob Crosby, but that fell through. Mum and Dad were a strong team at that time, and Dad was very dependent on Mum to look after everything while he worked very hard to forge a career in music."

Hollywood beckoned, and during this time, Nelson also took lessons from Italian composer Mario Castelnuovo-Tedesco who was forced to flee his native Florence in the late 1930's as World War Two threatened. Tedesco became a successful film composer in his own right, but in his early years in Hollywood, he was able to support his wife and two children by providing lessons in composition and symphonic orchestration to young, aspiring musicians seeking a career in films.

The process that Tedesco taught Nelson was to study a variety of piano pieces by classical composers such as Brahms, Schubert and Debussy, then get him to assign the voices or lines to the various sections or solo instruments on the orchestra. Nelson found this process invaluable later in his career, having to handle large groups of instruments. Nelson would later include the vocalist as an instrument to add to his deliberations when writing arrangements for large groups. He would also study with the classically trained Victor Bay, a former staff conductor at CBS. This would give Nelson the rudiments of conducting which he would draw on extensively throughout his management of large orchestras.

During this period of study with Tedesco and Bay, Nelson received income from writing arrangements for NBC Radio and working with Victor Young the songwriter and film score composer, famous for "My Foolish Heart" and "Shane" amongst many others.

Although he'd had a chequered career up to this point, the studious, industrious Nelson wasn't about to give up. He was doing arrangements, all uncredited; for example, in 1949, he wrote the arrangement for a Doris Day hit record titled "Again". This song was also covered by a twenty-one year old Vic Damone who earned a gold disc for his multi-million selling version the same year.

Nelson, with strong support from his wife, Doreen, continued to have that special inner belief that he could make something of himself. His reputation as a young, upcoming arranger was getting some attention and caught the eye of Les Baxter who was an orchestra leader at Capitol Records. Orchestra leaders at that time did not arrange music, although in Baxter's case he was one of the few that could write arrangements. The norm was that arrangements were passed to ghost writers. Nelson, for the time being at least, was to remain a ghost.

Studious Nelson 1940's. Photograph courtesy of Nelson Riddle Memorial Library Arizona State University.

Doreen and Nelson Riddle and their first car. Photograph courtesy of Christopher Riddle's personal collection.

3. UNFORGETTABLE

Unforgettable
In every way

In 1950, Les Baxter recruited Nelson Riddle to ghost-write some arrangements for Nat "King" Cole at Capitol Records. One of the songs was "Mona Lisa" which featured in a movie released in 1949 called *Captain Carey USA* starring Alan Ladd and Wanda Hendrix. "Mona Lisa" was sung in Italian and formed an important part of the plot as a secret code in relaying messages. The song became the first in a non-musical picture to win an academy award for best song. It was unexpected; the writers Ray Evans and Jay Livingston didn't even warrant a film credit as composers.

Nat and Nelson in tune. Photograph courtesy of Rosemary Acerra's personal collection.

Nelson plays, the children listen circa 1953. Rosemary (left)
Christopher (middle) Skip (right). Photograph courtesy of
Rosemary Acerra's personal collection.

Cole originally rejected the song as he plain didn't like
the tune. He thought it didn't fit his style one bit. He
referred to it as "that Italian song". Nonetheless, he was
encouraged by his producer Lee Gillette to cut a record.

Nelson took the opportunity given to him by Baxter
with both hands and wrote an enchanting arrangement
that transformed the song into a romantic love ballad.
Cole heard the arrangement, liked it, and agreed to
record it. But Cole had an inkling that this wasn't the
work of Les Baxter, although Baxter claimed full credit
and the record label shows "arranged and conducted by
Les Baxter".

When Cole was recording the song, he queried a music
note with the producer, asking whether a note was a B
flat or A sharp. The producer, Lee Gillette, deferred to
Baxter. When Cole saw Baxter conferring with Nelson,

it dawned on him that Baxter had not written the arrangement.

Christopher Riddle: "Nat saw my father and mother one afternoon in the studio: my mother copying some charts and my father writing furiously on his manuscript pad. Then the penny dropped with Nat who approached Dad and said, 'Les Baxter didn't write those arrangements. I'm guessing you did? I saw you running around in the fiddle section, but I thought you were the copyist.' My dad replied, 'Well, as matter of fact, Nat, my wife and I did do the copying, and it paid better than what I received for the arrangement!'"

There have been many cover versions of "Mona Lisa" spanning some fifty or sixty years, Andy Williams, Harry Connick Jr., and blues artist Little Willie Littlefield (no relation) among them. However, the definitive version is Cole's with Nelson's distinctively melodic arrangement, especially the use of the mandolin in the introduction and the ending. It was the best-selling song of 1950 and was inducted into the Grammy Hall of Fame in 1992.

Ray Evans and Jay Livingston, the composers, wrote: "Mona Lisa was the one for Nels. Not credited as the arranger, but that song kick-started his career. Nat found out that he did it, and of course, Nels went on to become a giant of the recording industry." Nelson's arrangement of "Too Young" followed the success of "Mona Lisa" and both became number one hits, after which Cole signed Nelson as his primary arranger.

The next big hit that followed had particular resonance. Christopher Riddle takes up the story: "My father was never credited on "Mona Lisa" or "Too Young"—Les Baxter took the credit but signing with Nat led to him being contracted by Capitol as their in-house arranger. He was now to be credited on each record—arranged and conducted by Nelson Riddle. The next song he did was aptly titled "Unforgettable" which turned out to be one of Nat's biggest hits, an evergreen that is still played to this very day".

Capitol Records was housed in the famous circular which is a 13-storey building designed by Louis Naidorf. It is one of the city's landmarks; construction began soon after EMI acquired Capitol Records in 1955, and work was completed in April 1956. It is situated slightly north of the Hollywood and Vine intersection. It has been described as the "world's first circular office building". The blinking light at the top of the tower spells out the word *Hollywood* in Morse code. The building is known as *The House That Nat Built* due to the vast numbers of records and amounts of merchandise that Nat Cole sold for the company.

Rosemary Acerra: "Dad's music caught on in the early 50's when he started working closely with Nat 'King' Cole. They both saw eye to eye and spent a lot of time in each other's company, aside from work. I got to know Cookie, Nat's wife, and Nat's daughter Natalie, who was nicknamed Sweetie. She and I took piano lessons together."

Until his working relationship with Nelson, Nat "King" Cole had generally been recognised as a jazz pianist and only latterly as a singer. Nelson provided Cole with lush, smooth orchestrations to match and showcase that equally lush, smooth vocal delivery which Cole possessed.

Nelson didn't care for others taking credit when credit wasn't due, as was the case with Baxter and other band leaders. It became a running sore with him. However, six years down the line, he managed to cure that particular ailment. Composer and conductor André Previn and Nelson were both working on different shows at NBC in Burbank, California. Their paths crossed one evening, so they decided to go for a coffee together before driving to their respective homes. As they walked further down the corridor, they saw Les Baxter walking towards them. Nelson confided in Previn that he couldn't stand Baxter. Previn empathised with Nelson but wanted to cool down a potentially explosive situation. A polite conversation followed between the three men ending with Baxter saying he had to turn out an arrangement overnight to meet a deadline.

Andre Previn: "Nelson nudged me and said, 'Les, what are friends for? I tell you what, let's the three of us go into that empty studio over there. I've got a lot of score paper with me. Now it's easy, I'll do the first third, André will do the second third, and you do the shout chorus. We'll be finished in an hour.'"

Baxter thanked his two colleagues but declined, saying, "I can't let you do that."

Nelson countered and asked for the name of tune and the key. Previn, at this time, was getting a little hot under the collar. Nelson and Previn completed their part of the arrangement, but Baxter after about five minutes, said, "Listen, this is crazy. I'm really grateful to you guys, but I'm going home to do my part."

Nelson turned on Baxter and said, "You do it right now!" Then Previn asked Baxter to see what he had written so far. He had written one bar for the woodwinds and the first note was a note for the oboe, one that doesn't exist on the instrument!

Previn drew that to Baxter's attention to which Baxter replied, "Oh, how silly. I meant that to be in the clarinets."

Nelson threw down the manuscript paper and said, "Oh, fuck off!" He and Previn left immediately and headed for the parking lot. Nelson told Previn that he couldn't stand a real fraud who steals credits. Previn had never seen Nelson so angry.

The moment Cole had realised that Nelson, not Les Baxter, was the man responsible for the orchestration of "Mona Lisa", he wanted to work and get to know the man behind the music. Cole's influence with Capitol was a game-changer for Nelson. The two men gelled musically and personally—the quiet, studious Nelson with the laid-back jazz pianist/singer.

Ella, Nat and Nelson. Photograph courtesy of Rosemary Acerra's personal collection.

Nelson putting finishing touches to his Gershwin album. Photograph
courtesy of Rosemary Acerra's personal collection.

Cole became intrigued by the art of musical arrangement
devoting a segment of his TV show to chronicle the
journey of the arrangement from conception on to
the copyist and then the vocalist. Cole and Nelson
became close, professionally and personally. Unlike
some of his peers, Cole didn't need to listen to an intro
of a song. A natural musician, he could go straight in—
he had perfect pitch.

The collaboration wasn't without its amusing side
stories. One weekend, there was a recording session
with Cole at Universal Studios in Chicago. A strange
sound could be heard while the musicians were having a
run through. An abrupt halt followed; the culprit was
identified: there was Nat "King" Cole sitting at the
back of the studio with a transistor radio listening to
baseball! He was a great fan, and his particular favourite
was Hank Aaron.

The Cole and Riddle families visited each other's homes
on a regular basis for social get-togethers. They saw

first-hand the racial abuse Cole received both in the neighbourhood and in the music business. When the Cole family moved to a new Hollywood home in Hancock Park, he was the subject of written objections from the local community, causing Cole to quip, "Given the way they have described me, I wouldn't want to live next door either." It became quite a frequent event for Cole's cars to be "keyed" and/or abusive notes affixed to the windscreen.

Despite good ratings, with an array of top guest stars and good reviews, *The Nat King Cole show* on NBC struggled to find a sponsor. NBC initially funded the production costs, and Nelson was musical director for 21 of the 27 episodes. However, no national sponsor came forward, many national corporations not wishing to upset their customers in the south who did not want to watch a black man in any other light than a subservient position. Although NBC was willing to continue to fund the production, Cole pulled out. In typically laid back and philosophical fashion, Cole shrugged his shoulders and said, "I guess Madison Avenue can't see in the dark."

Nat "King" Cole and Nelson Riddle recorded over 250 songs together from 1950 to 1960. There were many highlights, and while the two collaborators recorded single releases, there are a number of albums that merit attention. In 1956, *The Piano Style of Nat "King" Cole* released on Blue Note is one. This saw Cole in familiar vein as a jazz pianist; however, Nelson was commissioned to write orchestrations providing strings and brass in the best way to showcase Cole's gifts as a talented pianist.

The pair worked together on another five albums. *Nat King Cole Sings for Two in Love* was released on Capitol in 1955. *St. Louis Blues* was a biopic of W.C. Handy released in 1958. Cole played the lead role in the movie which Nelson scored. Cole sings Handy's repertoire of jazz and blues yet retained his aura as a pop star balladeer. This was Cole's only leading role in a major Hollywood film. Although W.C. Handy was a consultant on the film, he never lived to see it released. A soundtrack album produced by Lee Gillette on Capitol was in record stores five years later. Another hit single with Nat Cole was "Darling, Je Vous Aime Beaucoup" which reached number 7 on the Billboard chart. The song introduced in the film *Love and Hisses* in 1943, was recorded by Hildegarde and her version charted at number 21 the same year.

Cole Espanol was made with the Latin market in mind, part recorded in February 1958 in Havana and back at Capitol Records the following June in Los Angeles. The album reached no. 12 on the Billboard magazine chart and was inducted into the Latin Hall of Fame in 2007.

Next followed *To Whom It May Concern*, all new ballads released on Capitol in 1959. There were three bonus tracks included on a CD re-issue. The year 1960 brought their last album together, titled *Wild Love.* This was a concept album that told a story about the search for love. It was nominated for a Grammy for Album of the Year in 1961, losing out to Bob Newhart's *The Button-Down Mind of Bob Newhart.*

After the release of that album, the two of them were not to work together again, partly a result of Nelson spending most of his time collaborating with Frank Sinatra. Nat and Nelson never fell out over that, and they remained friends right up until Cole's untimely death from lung cancer five years later. Nelson visited Cole at the St John's hospital supplying Cole with the various comic-books he loved to read. The two men had been through some truly unforgettable experiences together, both in a professional and personal capacity.

In tribute to his friend and colleague, Nelson released an instrumental album on the Reprise label in 1966, a year after Cole had passed away—the album's producer was Sonny Burke. It was titled simply *Nat - an orchestral portrait of Nat "King" Cole*.

4. TOO MARVELLOUS FOR WORDS

It's all too wonderful
I'll never find the words

"Nelson had a fresh approach to orchestration, and I made myself fit into what he was doing." Frank Sinatra

Sinatra was quiet, listening with intent. The producers waited; no-one knew what to expect as he was notoriously unpredictable. The wait was worth it. "Who wrote that one? It's a gasser!"

"He did," (pointing to Nelson Riddle) was the unanimous reply.

In 1952, Frank Sinatra was playing to empty rooms. His producer at Columbia, Mitch Miller, said at the time they "couldn't give away" Sinatra's records.

"He's a dead man," the talent agent Irving "Swifty" Lazar declared. "Even Jesus couldn't get resurrected in this town."

This decline led to financial difficulties, exacerbated by his divorce to wife Nancy. It was also at this time he was having an affair with actress Ava Gardner. He would go on to marry Gardner, but it was a tempestuous period, and emotional stress always had an adverse effect on Sinatra's pipes.

The following year, head of Columbia Pictures, Harry Cohn, was casting the movie *From Here to Eternity.* The film was to be based on James Jones's 1951 best-selling novel. Sinatra was aware of the story and felt the role of Private Angelo Maggio was meant for him. He related to the role and identified with the character from his own experience as a kid living in Hoboken, New Jersey. Sinatra literally begged Cohn to cast him as Maggio. Cohn didn't feel he was right for the part, but Sinatra wouldn't give up. Telegram after telegram was sent to Cohn all signed off, "Maggio", pleading for a screen test. Meanwhile, Ava Gardner worked on Cohn's wife, Joan. Cohn eventually relented but only after Sinatra agreed to take a relatively meagre salary of $8,000.

Only seven years earlier, Sinatra had been able to command a fee of $150,000 for *Anchors Aweigh* starring alongside Gene Kelly. Accepting such a lowly fee for playing Maggio was a gamble but one that he had total belief would pay off.

That confidence was borne out, as the film was an enormous box office and critical success winning eight Oscars, one of those for Sinatra as Best Supporting Actor. He was back, as an actor at least. From 1952, Nelson Riddle's burgeoning reputation as an arranger was making recording executives sit up and take notice. Conversely, Sinatra's record deal with Columbia Records wasn't renewed. However, Capitol Records took a chance and signed Sinatra. A calculated risk, they wanted to create a new Sinatra, not just a balladeer, but a swinger with a new fresh sound. Sinatra didn't balk at that idea but insisted that he would stick with his erstwhile arranger Axel Stordahl, whereas Capitol wanted him to form a new collaboration with Nelson Riddle. Stordahl's response was to write some new arrangements for Capitol which were fine, but they didn't usher in a new era.

Capitol insisted that Sinatra try the new way and asked Nelson to do a couple of songs in Billy May's style and two of his own. Sinatra listened to May's "South of the Border" which he liked but really came round to the idea once he'd heard Nelson's arrangement of "I've Got The World on a String"; he knew there and then he had found a special collaborator. Sinatra was blown away by the seismic change in musical direction, and it was musical migration he was keen to undertake.

What happened next defined American popular music over the next decade. The Sinatra/Riddle collaboration delivered concept albums par excellence, best sellers in the field.

As is often the case, there are conflicting stories on how the Sinatra/Riddle union first came about. Sinatra was filmed in the movie *That's Entertainment 2* saying that he had followed Nelson's work with Nat Cole and wanted to work with Nelson "to see if they could do something special". He continued very much tongue-in-cheek, commenting, "I never did hear whether it worked out or not."

Nelson "Skip" Riddle III recalls: "I used to enjoy watching Frank work in the studio, great to see Dad also. There was great sensitivity on his part. He gave the orchestra players very little slack, but Dad knew his place and was extremely respectful to Frank and other singers he worked with, like Ella and Nat. This was an art in itself to get the artist to fully express themselves."

The Sinatra Music Society:

"Sinatra and Riddle, like Laurel and Hardy, stick together like glue. In the bi-annual polls in our magazine *Perfectly Frank*, top of the charts in Best Album

(Ballads) section was invariably *In the Wee Small Hours of the Morning* and top of the Best Album (Up Tempo) section was always *Songs for Swingin' Lovers*.

"Our society was formed at just around the time that the Sinatra/Riddle tour de force started. The wonderfully constructed orchestrations formed the perfect background to the mature Sinatra sound. The duo went on to record around twenty ground-breaking albums for the Capital and Reprise labels. In Sinatra's world, 'Genius meets Genius.'" – David Smith

Nelson started to work with Sinatra. In contrast to the easy-going, close relationship he had with Nat Cole, his relationship with Sinatra was wholly different. Whilst both of them shared a love of music, Nelson found Sinatra tense and unpredictable, yet always very business-like. Over the years, Nelson had developed a skill for writing copious notes quickly, yet they were always legible when he re-visited them, sometimes weeks later. This kept him in good stead for his many discussions with Sinatra when planning an up-coming album. The accuracy of those discussions was important, as the album could be several months away in the making, and Nelson was unlikely to reprise the discussion with Sinatra in the same way because of the singer's busy schedule.

Nelson found the planning discussions with Sinatra to be mentally very taxing to the point of headache and pulse racing. Sinatra would bombard him with very specific and long-winded detail of what he wanted on the first few tunes, citing many classical composers as examples of what he was looking for. After one or two hours of discussions along these lines, Sinatra started to wane and the conversation about the remaining songs (most albums consisting of twelve songs in those days) was much more generic, with Sinatra often signing off by saying, "Do what you think best, Nelson."

Christopher Riddle: "My father and Frank Sinatra are often mentioned in the same breath. It was back in 1953 that their musical marriage started. Sinatra was always specific that a really great song was only as good as its arrangement. I was to find myself in Frank's company on many occasions. He got to call me by my first name!"

Their partnership was not just confined to recording albums, they also worked on movies, television extravaganzas, and live dates.

Our Town, Nelson rehearses with Paul Newman and Eva-Marie Saint.
Photograph courtesy of Rosemary Acerra's personal collection.

Songs For Swingin' Lovers Photograph courtesy
Capitol Records (Universal Music)

Our Town was written by Thornton Wilder. Sinatra
played the central role as a stage manager. This
production was to be a 90-minute special for NBC—a
musical take on the successful stage play. It was agreed
at the onset that Nelson would arrange and conduct but
when Nelson visited Sinatra's apartment a few days
later, Sinatra told Nelson that NBC had hired a conductor
from Chicago, but it was ok because he could still do
the arrangements. Nelson was dismayed but didn't hold
back and let Sinatra know of his deep disappointment.
Sinatra said there was little he could do as the show was
due to air in the next six days. However, Sinatra clearly
sensed Nelson's displeasure so excused himself and
went in the next room to make a phone call. After a few
minutes, he came back to say all had been sorted, and
Nelson would arrange and conduct. He added that
Nelson better get over to Burbank studios double quick
as there was only a few days left before airtime! Nelson

appreciated the fact that Sinatra went out on a limb for him and would cite this and other occasions to demonstrate the loyalty displayed by the singer.

Aside from Sinatra, the cast included up and coming actors Paul Newman and Eva-Marie Saint. The latter was to go on and play opposite Cary Grant in Hitchcock's movie classic *North By North West*. Sammy Cahn and Jimmy Van Heusen wrote the title song for *Our Town* and the memorable tune "Love and Marriage", for which Nelson's arrangement included a vibrant tuba section. Cahn, who was the lyricist of the song, was awarded an Emmy.

As was the norm in those days, this was a live show; however, the ninety-minute performance went by without incident. Nelson received an Emmy nomination. The loyalty Sinatra paid back to Nelson had reaped rewards but sadly the show was never recorded, so there is no footage available.

"Half of Frank's success during his golden period was down to Nelson." – André Previn.

Christopher Riddle: "Frank had the highest respect for my father and vice-versa. He deferred to Dad regularly. This is mostly illustrated by the introductions and endings of the songs, effectively my dad's signature. He used to say, 'I set it up and get the hell out of the way when Frank sings.' My father trained his ear over many years and composed marvellous countermelodies that underscored the song. All these ingredients and Frank's masterful phrasing and interpretation meant that their collaboration was unrivalled in American popular music."

Sinatra's respect and admiration was far greater than Nelson ever realised. *In the Wee Small Hours* released in 1955 was rated by many as one of the greatest ever albums. Sinatra was so thrilled with Nelson's arrangement of "What Is This Thing Called Love", he turned to the studious, cheerless arranger and said, "Nelson, you're a gas!" It was Sinatra's highest compliment. There was a pregnant pause while the less than spontaneous Nelson came up with the best response he could think of. "Likewise," he said.

To truly understand the tremendous impact the Sinatra/Riddle collaboration made let's take an in depth look at some of the other concept albums they created. *Songs For Swingin' Lovers* is a good place to start.

There was an uplifting mood on the whole album and the combination between the two masters meant that every song took on a new meaning. For example, "I've Got You Under My Skin" was never a significant composition of the Cole Porter songbook—not until these two got hold of it; then it was completely transformed from a non-entity ballad into a swinging affair which remains at the pinnacle of important songs which makes up the *Great American Songbook*.

AllMusic's review of *Songs For Swingin' Lovers*:

"After the ballad-heavy *In the Wee Small Hours,* Frank Sinatra and Nelson Riddle returned to up-tempo, swing material with *Songs for Swingin' Lovers*; arguably Sinatra's greatest swing set. Like Sinatra's previous Capitol albums, *Songs for Swingin' Lovers* consists of re-interpreted pop standards, ranging from the ten-year-old "You Make Me Feel So Young" to the 20-year-old "Pennies From Heaven" and "I've Got You Under My Skin." Sinatra is supremely confident throughout the album, singing with authority and joy. That joy is replicated in Riddle's arrangements, which manage to rethink these standards in fresh yet reverent ways. Working with a core rhythm section and a full string orchestra, Riddle writes scores that are surprisingly subtle. "I've Got You Under My Skin," with its breathtaking middle section, is a perfect example of how Sinatra works with the band. Both swing hard, stretching out the rhythms and melodies but never losing sight of the original song. *Songs for Swingin' Lovers!* never loses momentum. The great songs keep coming and the performances are all stellar, resulting in one of Sinatra's true classics.

"It's a Swinging Affair! could be considered the sequel album to *Swingin' Lovers.* In some ways, *It's A Swingin' Affair!* is *Songs for Swingin' Lovers!* part 2, following the same formula of Sinatra's hit album of the previous year. Beneath the surface, there are enough variations on *A Swingin' Affair!* to make it a distinctive and equally enjoyable listen. The most noticeable difference between the two records is their basic approach. Where *Songs for Swingin' Lovers!* swung hard but managed to stay rather light, *A Swingin' Affair!* is a forceful, brassy album—it exudes a self-assured, confident aura. It is a hard, brash, jazzy album."

Just before Nelson began work on arranging the songs for *Only The Lonely,* his six-month-old daughter, Leonora Celeste, had died from bronchial asthma. Frank and Nelson went into the studio on 5 May 1958 to begin work on the album, but none of the three songs that were cut were used. Nelson's mother was critically ill, and it can only have affected the session. She died four days later.

At the time of the recording, Sinatra's divorce from Ava Gardner had been finalized.

Nelson remarked: "If I can attach events like that to music, perhaps *Only the Lonely* was the result."

The content of that album is Nelson's favourite, as he had more leeway to express himself.

AllMusic Review:

"Certainly it is considered to have Nelson's greatest collection of arrangements under one roof and the most emotionally charged involvement, rarely exhibited in other works. The sombre mood throughout was perhaps reflective of the two collaborator's feelings at the time. *Only The Lonely* remained on the Billboard chart in the US for an astounding 120 weeks. Ask people to name Sinatra's saddest album and most will say, *In The Wee Small Hours Of The Morning*, but *Sinatra Sings For Only The Lonely* is probably more sad. It's undeniably a masterpiece."

As noted in Peter Levinson's book *September In The Rain*:

"Nelson chose several instrumental soloists to communicate the essence of the music on the album. Harry Edison showed the sombre side of his playing on 'Willow Weep for Me'. The trombonist, Ray Sims, delivered the finest recording work of his long career with two meaningful solos and Bill Miller contributed several beautiful piano solos."

Three weeks later, Frank returned to the studio, and while the arrangements for the album were Nelson's, it was Felix Slatkin who conducted the orchestra before Nelson returned for the last two sessions that completed the album. Both Nelson and Sinatra conceded that it was their favourite album, yet it was conceived in exceptionally sad circumstances.

Young At Heart Photograph Warner Bros.

The Joker is Wild aka All The Way Photograph
courtesy Paramount Pictures.

On the film front, *Young at Heart,* released in 1954, isn't strictly a film credit for Nelson, but his influence is there for all to hear. Actually, Nelson had introduced Sinatra to the title song.

Sinatra recalled, "Nelson told me he had a song that had been floating around Vine Street [Capitol Records] and other companies for weeks or months.

"'I think it's a good song,' Nelson said, 'but nobody wants to do it.' I didn't even ask him if I could hear it. I just said let's do it, and it turned out to be "Young at Heart". We did a single, and it was a big hit." Source: *Frank Sinatra: An American Legend by Nancy Sinatra.*

The making of the film was not without internal dramas. Sinatra didn't warm to co-star Doris Day's husband, Martin Melcher, who was on set every day. He felt Melcher was using Day as a vehicle for his own ends and had him banned from the production. After Melcher's death some fourteen years later, it was revealed that he had frittered away all the money Day had made during a twenty-year film career. Sinatra also fell out with the director of photography, Charles Lang. Sinatra, as we know, was loath to rehearse, and he was put out by the meticulous Lang's setting up of camera shots and penchant for repeated takes. Sinatra walked off set threatening to quit the film. Lang was fired and replaced by Ted McCord.

On a more convivial note, Ethel Barrymore who appeared as Aunt Jessie in the film, was given a lavish surprise birthday party by Sinatra. She was in frail health during filming and in between shots had to use a wheelchair. She was greatly moved by this impromptu and warm gesture.

Young At Heart had a different title when in development but such was the success of the song on the hit parade that the producers re-named the film title after the song. There are other Riddle arrangements used during the film, including the classic Sinatra bar-room song, a Harold Arlen composition, "One For My Baby". The film co-starred Gig Young as Alex Burke. Nelson was to work with him some ten years later on the TV series *The Rogues*.

Sinatra's character, Barney Sloan, is a down at heel musician who finds love with Doris Day's character, Laurie, who breaks off her engagement to the suave, sophisticated Burke to marry Barney. Such was Sinatra's newfound influence, they changed the ending of the film at his request. Barney's attempt at suicide was meant to be fatal, but the storyline was changed to his survival and newfound happiness with Laurie.

Young At Heart is a musical drama, un-ashamedly sentimental and perfectly suited to a Sunday afternoon viewing; a film that keeps movie fans entertained by top notch acting and marvellous music.

Release dates for films do not necessarily reflect the development phase or the production date, whilst it might appear that they are year on year releases. Sinatra and Riddle were often in the recording studios between films. Their different roles in the film-making process, however, meant that Sinatra as a film star would be working long periods on set whereby Nelson's role in writing the score would invariably be carried out during the post-production process, i.e., when the final footage has been edited. It is then that any overtures and incidental music can be applied.

Christopher Riddle: "'Young at Heart' was different. It was a ballad, but it was a 'playful' ballad. It had a very wide appeal because of the style of it. Dad was about 32 years old when he came up with that arrangement. 'Don't Worry 'Bout Me' is another one; both have a lot of depth in them. He had a remarkable musical memory. Everything he heard went into a library in his head, and he drew from it. He would take people aside from each section of the band, for example the woodwind, and ask what is the best range to write for this instrument? He was the perpetual student."

The movie *Guys and Dolls,* which was released in 1955, tested Sinatra's patience to the limit. Marlon Brando, much to Sinatra's chagrin, was cast as Sky Masterson, and Sinatra played Nathan Detroit. He must have agonised over Brando's rendition of "Luck be a Lady". Sinatra recorded it later with great success and used it regularly in his stage show. Having been overlooked for other parts that went to Brando, it rankled with Sinatra, and the two never got on. For instance, Sinatra was well known for not liking re-takes. He preferred his first take every time. Brando, however, was the antithesis of Sinatra, who was heard to comment, "When Mumbles is through rehearsing, I'll come out."

The MGM production of *The Tender Trap* was a movie release the same year, which was the year CBS introduced the iconic quiz show the *64,000 Dollar Question*. Nelson didn't write the score for this movie, but if I was to write a review, my centre piece would be the title song "The Tender Trap". It epitomises the Riddle arrangements for Sinatra with its distinctive yet easy, swinging style. The film, directed by Charles "Chuck" Walters, had Debbie Reynolds starring opposite Sinatra and had a screen debut for a young James Drury who later found fame as TV's *The Virginian*. I actually got to know James Drury quite well in recent years.

"Jim" was always very affable and approachable. He and I were due to collaborate on producing a western movie titled *Men of The West,* but he sadly passed before we could make that happen.

That same year saw the release of *Johnny Concho,* an offbeat western. It didn't really do it for me. The screenplay was quite bizarre and Sinatra appeared miscast. Nelson's title theme "Wait for Me" is the best thing in the movie. This was the first film produced by Sinatra.

In 1957, Sinatra was given his own show by ABC television. Nelson was assigned to do the arrangements which would include Sinatra singing with various guest artists, show by show. This operation was to be a highly complicated affair as Sinatra insisted he would film and sing with only his rhythm section, with the rest of the orchestra to be added later. Nelson had to add the orchestra and record the music with the film running alongside the faint sound of the rhythm section accompanying Sinatra. The tempo of the rhythm section's "ups" and "downs" was difficult to follow. Nelson's task was to make it seem like it sounded that it was all done at the same time with one orchestra! However, calamity struck and the whole process had to be re-scored due to the fact Nelson had not tuned the orchestra to Sinatra's voice before starting recording. There was, therefore, a total mis-match. Fearing the worst, Nelson expected to be fired, yet the unpredictable, mostly loyal Sinatra told Nelson to re-score the shows, and this time tune up to his voice! To Nelson's relief that's exactly what he did.

Christopher Riddle: "It was around this time that my father put Bill Miller as Sinatra's piano player and Irv Cottler on drums, the reason being Frank would often tour with just a quintet. Putting these two guys in there would give a consistency to his performance. A side story: there was a restaurant in Hollywood at the time called Sorrento's, and if you booked a table, you may well have found Bill playing piano. He loved to play regardless of the occasion. Imagine back in the day, you book a dinner date and get to hear Bill Miller play for free."

One of my favourite movies is the 1957 release *The Joker is Wild*. This film provides Sinatra with an ideal platform to show his considerable acting skills. A true story, he plays Joe E. Lewis, a singer who has his vocal chords severed by a mobster. The soundtrack of the movie includes the classic "All The Way". Nelson gets out of the way and his subtle arrangements let the marvellous Sinatra vocals do the rest. Not a dry eye in the house.

The song, with Nelson's orchestral arrangement, won the Best Song Oscar for Jimmy Van Heusen and Sammy Cahn. It also made the top of the charts both sides of the Atlantic. Mysteriously, Sinatra was overlooked in the best actor nominations. When the film was re-released, it was re-titled *All The Way* after the success of the Oscar winning song.

Taller than the tallest tree is
That's how it's got to feel

The same year saw another iconic movie release, *Pal Joey*. This was a long time in development because of conflicting schedules over casting the film. The original choice as director was the brilliant Billy Wilder. He had discussed the possibility of directing at a restaurant with the notorious head of Columbia Pictures, Harry Cohn. Cohn turned down Wilder's advances but not only

Pal Joey Photograph courtesy of Paramount Pictures

Can Can Photograph Twentieth Century Fox

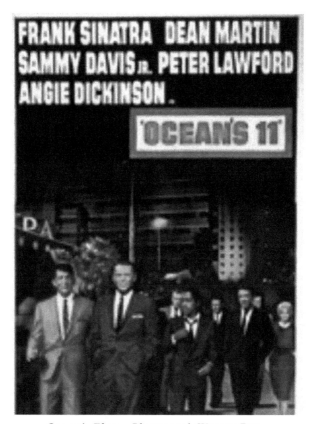

Ocean's Eleven Photograph Warner Bros.

that, he sent Wilder the bill for lunch! Eventually, the director was named as George Sidney, who directed Stewart Granger in *Scaramouche*. The delectable Rita Hayworth and Kim Novak were cast to play the female leads. Sinatra was cast as Hayworth's toy boy yet in real life she was three years younger than him. The film is a light musical comedy and is best remembered for the introduction of the song "The Lady is a Tramp", the electrifying, up tempo classic which is now an indelible part of our musical memory.

The movie *A Hole in The Head* has an array of star actors starring opposite Sinatra, such as Edward G.

Robinson, Carolyn Jones, Keenan Wynn to name but three. The stand-out song is "High Hopes" recorded by Sinatra with a "bunch of kids". On one recording session, that bunch of kids was to include Christopher and Rosemary Riddle (Acerra) who also sang as part of the Jimmy Joyce singers on a "Pocketful of Miracles", another Sinatra song which was the title of a Glenn Ford/Bette Davis movie. "High Hopes" was to win the 1960 Oscar for Best Music, Original Song for Jimmy Van Heusen and Sammy Cahn. The arrangement has that distinctive Nelson Riddle sound.

Squeezed in between those two movies was the release of *High Society,* a musical re-make of *The Philadelphia Story*. Here Sinatra stars opposite his idol, Bing Crosby, and Grace Kelly. Although Sinatra and Crosby had appeared together in a number of radio and television shows, they had always wanted to do a movie together. The right project hadn't turned up until *High Society.* Even then the producers realised late in the day that the pair didn't have a musical number together. Who can forget the wonderfully orchestrated and choreographed duet of Crosby and Sinatra for "Well Did You Evah?" It was a swell party, as Nelson shared orchestration duties with Conrad Salinger.

In the year 1960, Kennedy beat Nixon to the White House by the slimmest of margins. It also heralded another movie score for Nelson. The Twentieth Century Fox release *Can Can* was a French musical comedy which saw Sinatra perform alongside Shirley MacLaine and legendary French actor, Maurice Chevalier. During filming, Soviet President Nikita Khrushchev visited the set with his wife, Nina, and was shocked at what he saw, condemning the film as pornographic and depraved, saying "the face of mankind is prettier than its back-side."

Although the film garnered another Oscar nomination for Nelson for Best Music, Scoring of a Musical Picture, he was unsuccessful once again having lost the previous year for *L'il Abner*. Ironically, this time he lost out to *Song Without End*. However, *Can Can* did win a Grammy for the Best Soundtrack Album.

The Cole Porter composed songs included "Let's Do It (Let's Fall in Love)", "C'est Magnifique" and "Montmart". Porter's immortal hit, "I Love Paris", is strangely absent as a vocal rendition, although it is fully utilised by Nelson as an underscore theme in the "Adam and Eve" ballet scene.

Nelson scored a number of movies in sixties that starred the *Rat Pack*, an informal group of entertainers, namely Sinatra, Peter Lawford, Dean Martin, Joey Bishop, and Sammy Davis Jr. who performed together with a guest star or two.

First, there was *Ocean's Eleven* released in 1960. Danny Ocean (Sinatra) gathers a group of his WW2 buddies to pull off a Las Vegas heist by robbing five casinos in one night. Billy Wilder (*Double Indemnity, Lost Weekend, Sunset Boulevard*) worked on the script as a favour to Sinatra. For his troubles, Sinatra gave him a sketch by Pablo Picasso.

During this production, Sammy Davis Jr. was forced to stay in a "coloureds only" hotel, despite appearing on stage with the other clan members at the Sands Hotel. Outraged, Frank Sinatra confronted the casino owners and Davis was allowed to stay at the major hotel; this was ground-breaking at the time as it broke Las Vegas's unofficial colour bar. There is a famous scene in the final shot of the film where the eleven walk past the sign at the front of the Sands hotel, the five *Rat Pack* members of the cast are billed on the sign. The movie soundtrack includes Nelson's distinctive arrangements of "Ain't That a Kick In the Head" (Martin), "Eee-0-11" (Davis Jr.) and instrumental versions of "The Tender Trap" and "Learnin' The Blues".

Christopher Riddle: "I was very fortunate as I got to go back to Frank's house and hang out with him on occasions, as my dad would often visit Frank's place in Cherokee Lane.

"In fact, that is the house they used to film *Ocean's Eleven*. Whilst my dad and Frank were talking music business in the house, I was lazing by the pool! Frank had a Japanese houseboy at the time, and he used to bring refreshments and food out to the pool. Frank was a very genial host, always concerned that his guests had enough of everything. I often say to today's audiences that I started at the top and am working my way down and enjoying great success in achieving that. Seriously, I have been very fortunate to have played and backed so many iconic singers."

An English born actor, the aristocratic Peter Lawford who had been friends with Sinatra since the late 1940's was an early member of Sinatra's *Rat Pack*. This group had originally been formed by Humphrey Bogart and named the *Holmby Hills Rat-Pack* by his wife Lauren Bacall. The group included founder members such as David Niven, Errol Flynn, Spencer Tracy, and Cary Grant. Sinatra acquired the description in the 60's when the media dubbed him and his cohorts the new *Rat Pack*.

I first remember Lawford starring as the lead in *The Thin Man* TV series which ran from 1957 to 1959, where he reprised the part of amateur sleuth Nick Charles. The role was made famous on the big screen by William Powell.

Lawford was cultivated further by Sinatra as he had become an influential member of the Kennedy family by marrying John F. Kennedy's sister Patricia. Sinatra was fascinated by politics and the power and influence it exerted. Lawford was a very useful ally to Sinatra who was backing the young senator from Massachusetts to become the next president of the United States in his run-off with the then vice-president Richard Nixon.

The Sinatra/Lawford axis was beneficial to Nelson too, as political affiliations and film productions would afford Nelson plenty of opportunities to weave his unique musicality into film scores and also as part of political rally's stage management. Lawford had become something of a "fixer" for Sinatra who had always been attracted by Lawford's perfect English diction, enunciation and elan. Lawford had his brother-in-law's ear; in fact, Sinatra had nicknamed him Brother-in-Lawford.

Sinatra had in turn become very useful to JFK as he could help bring the trade union's vote behind the Democrat party candidate, having good connections with the union financial backers albeit some were of dubious character. Sinatra had grown up with these guys in the neighbourhood, but there was no evidence whatsoever of wrongdoing on his part. However, the budding relationship with JFK, like most political relationships, ended in tears. Sinatra helped deliver the White House for Kennedy, but in return, Kennedy delivered a perceived snub to Sinatra by opting to stay with Bing Crosby, a lifelong Republican, rather than with Sinatra who had gone to great lengths to customise his Palm Springs residence in anticipation of President Kennedy's stay.

Sinatra blamed Lawford who quickly became persona non-grata and was immediately banished from the Rat

Pack. Sinatra only spoke to Lawford on one other occasion in 1963 after Frank Sinatra Jr. had been kidnapped. Sinatra sought Lawford's help in putting him in touch with Robert F. Kennedy, JFK's brother and the then attorney general.

The year 1963 saw *Come Blow Your Horn* released in cinemas. It was in the top twenty highest grossing films that year. Based on a Neil Simon play, Nelson's score was well received, and the soundtrack album was a commercial success. The title song sung by Sinatra was the only musical number in the picture.

The same year, another movie, *Four for Texas,* was released, a comedy western starring Sinatra and Dean Martin, directed by Robert Aldrich. Aldrich didn't care much for Sinatra's working style and wanted him replaced. It may have been to do with Sinatra not being keen to do more than one take. This contrasted, as previously stated, to his multiple-take work ethic in the recording studio. The production company was SAM which stood for Sinatra and Martin, the two stars had partnered up with Warner Bros for distribution. There was a cameo appearance for The Three Stooges, which just about sums it all up.

Robin and the 7 Hoods, released the following year, was altogether a much superior affair. Nelson's score was nominated for an Academy Award in 1965, losing out to his friend and colleague André Previn who won for *My Fair Lady.* There is a star-studded cast. As well as Sinatra there is Bing Crosby, Dean Martin, Sammy Davis Jr., Peter Falk (Columbo) and Edward G. Robinson. Barbara Rush provides the glamorous humour as the maid "Marian". The characters' names were loosely aligned to those in Robin Hood, for example, Robbo, Alan A. Dale, Guy Gisborne, etc. Peter Lawfordwas originally cast as Alan A. Dale, but, ironically, he was replaced by Bing Crosby following Lawford's big

625 Ocean Front
Santa Monica
California

February 7, 1961

Mr. Nelson Riddle
3853 Carbon Canyon Road
Malibu, California

Dear Nelson,

First of all let me say thank you on behalf of the
Democratic National Committee, all of the Kennedys, Frank
Sinatra and myself for your marvelous contribution to the
Inaugural Gala in Washington.

As far as I am concerned there will never again be a
night like it and it will long be one of my most cherished
memories.

The most gratifying experience to evolve from the evening, second only to the President's extraordinary words of
praise regarding our profession, was the terrific interest
generated throughout the country by various Democratic organ-
izations whose members were unable to attend the event, but
who had the knowledge that we had taped the show and who are
now clamoring to see it. You will be delighted to hear that
Roger Edens and Bill Asher did a superb job on the taping
itself and we are all extremely pleased with it.

I am sure you are aware that on the evening of January
nineteenth we raised better than $1,400,000, but the fact
remains that the existing deficit stands at $2,200,000.
After the initial shock of this staggering figure, there
was born an idea: to lease the tape to the aforementioned
Democratic groups from coast to coast on a closed circuit
basis at a fee to be decided upon according to the area,
with all the proceeds reverting directly to the Democratic
National Committee.

Letter from Peter Lawford. Copy courtesy of the
Nelson Riddle Memorial Library Arizona State University.

Mr. Nelson Riddle   2.   February 7, 1961

An idea also evolved to sell it to television for one ninety minute spectacular in the near future. The benefits from this project would also revert directly to the Democratic National Committee.

In closing, the two projections which I have discussed have a rough estimated return of better than $2,000,000, according to Matthew McCloskey, Finance Chairman for the Committee.

Your release for this venture will be invaluable. The decision is yours.

"There will now be a ten minute intermission."

Most sincerely,

Peter Lawford

PL/ja

P.S. Enclosed please find a formal release for your perusal and the benefit of your lawyers.

P.L.

Letter from Peter Lawford part two. courtesy of the Nelson Riddle Memorial Library Arizona State University.

fall out with Sinatra. Nelson used "My Kind of Town" as the orchestral opening and in the closing credits, whilst Sinatra sings it as the film's centre-piece vocal. The actual filming took place between Oct and Dec 1963 but was marred by the assassination of President Kennedy.

President John F. Kennedy inauguration 1961
Thank you letter. Courtesy of Christopher Riddle personal collection.

Robin and the 7 Hoods recording session Bing sings, Dino deals.
Nelson and the children look on. Photograph courtesy of
Rosemary Acerra's personal collection.

Robin and 7 Hoods film poster. Courtesy Warner Bros.

Christopher Riddle: "Skip, Rosemary and I went along with our father to one of the recording sessions where Bing and Dean were performing. We were out there at Warner's for the recording of the music for *Robin and the 7 Hoods*. I went a number of times to observe the underscoring and used to hang out in the green room and go to lunch with them, and also helped out in Frank's office (he had an office at Warner Bros). His production company at the time was Seven Arts. I was 13 years old."

Nelson was musical director for Sinatra on many live performances during this period. There were two standout live US performances with the Tommy Dorsey Orchestra at the Paramount Theatre in 1956 following the making of the movie *Johnny Concho,* where the audience described Sinatra's performance as scintillating.

There was television too. One memorable show in 1965 was *Frank Sinatra: A Man and His Music* which many regard as the ultimate TV music special. It marked Sinatra's 50th birthday. Nelson shared orchestration duties with Gordon Jenkins. The show won the Emmy Award for *Outstanding Music Programme,* and there was an album release which won the Grammy Award for *Album of the Year* in 1967. Such was the success of the programme, NBC commissioned two sequels *A Man and His Music – Part II, featuring Nancy Sinatra. A Man and His Music* broadcast in 1966. *A Man and His Music + Ella + Jobim* which co-starred *First Lady of Jazz,* Ella Fitzgerald, and *The King of Bossa Nova,* Antonio Carlos Jobim, was served by Nelson and his orchestra. The programme consisted of a number of solo performances and duet medleys of Sinatra/Jobim and Sinatra/Fitzgerald. These shows were followed by other specials such as *Francis Albert Sinatra Does his Thing* (1968), *Sinatra* (1969) and following his return out of retirement, *Ol' Blue Eyes is Back* (18th November 1973).

The last movie score Nelson did with Sinatra was *Marriage On The Rocks* in 1965. It was a romantic comedy co-starring Dean Martin and Deborah Kerr. This is not a musical film despite the presence of Sinatra and Martin. Nancy Sinatra appeared in the movie and was quite nervous acting opposite her father. She was also going through a divorce from her first husband, Tommy Sands. This movie was not a happy experience for her.

A hit-back album for Sinatra in 1966 was *Strangers in the Night.* Nelson was reluctant to do the album because he did not write the arrangement to the title track, which was Ernie Freeman's arrangement. The label wanted to do the album off the back of the success of the single; however, Nelson relented and arranged and

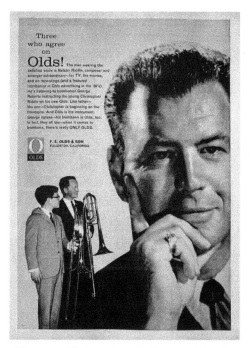

Like father, like son. Christopher, Nelson and the legendary bass trombonist George Roberts advertise Olds trombones. Photograph courtesy Christopher Riddle's personal collection.

Christopher Riddle and Dean Martin. Robin and the 7 Hoods recording session 1963. Photograph courtesy of Christopher Riddle's personal collection.

conducted the remaining tracks on the album. Standout tracks are "Summer Wind", the arrangement of which Nelson used an organ in his opening.

After working a concert with Betty Hutton in 1954, Nelson went to a bar and heard Wild Bill Davis playing and became fascinated by the organ. No arranger had used an organ in an orchestration for Sinatra before. It took Nelson twelve years to implement. Nelson was very pleased with his arrangement of "Summer Wind" which is rare in itself because he was always seeking perfection. He computed that Sinatra was pleased too, because there was no adverse comment. Nelson's arrangement of "All or Nothing at All" is another showstopper. The bonus tracks added to the album include a live concert where Sinatra refers to this old song he used to sing when he was with Harry James. Nelson's arrangement is something else, truly something special as Sinatra acknowledges on the record. There are other old favourites such as "Downtown", a Tony Hatch penned hit for Petula Clark. Sinatra's version is altogether different, I will say no more.

Nelson expanded on his relationship with Sinatra in an interview with Jonathan Schwartz from 1983: "Sinatra picked all of the songs himself. He was conversant with classical music, and he would give me various examples. He would say I want this kind of a sound here and this kind of a sound there."

A visit to the library was the first stop after Sinatra requested a "Puccini" sound backing to Nelson, as Nelson had never studied the operatic scores. Vocalising as a cultivated singing voice as evidenced in operas was repellent to Nelson. He had to gen up on Puccini and others in order to understand Sinatra's request.

"I'm not sure Nelson" Sammy Davis Jr ponders Nelson's arrangement
while Bing and Dean chill out. Photograph courtesy of Christopher
Riddle's personal collection.

Sinatra and the man behind the music. The White House 1973. Photograph
courtesy of Rosemary Acerra's personal collection.

Sinatra was always very clear in mapping out want he wanted, where the crescendo should take place, and where the diminuendo came in. The discussions could be painful because they were so detailed and went on for considerable time; it became very intense. Nelson learned a lot, however, from these discussions even if he may have lost his rag after leaving the studio. He learned the importance of tempos, the dynamics, and he constructed his orchestrations to breathe with Sinatra, phrase by phrase.

In the mid-seventies, Sinatra commissioned some new all string charts from Nelson to be featured during the ballad part of his performances, usually after about three up-tempo tunes at the beginning. Nelson contributed "Imagination", "What's New", "My Funny Valentine", "Spring is Here", "You Go To My Head", and "Embraceable You". These were, of course, different from Nelson's previous charts for Frank during the Capitol recording sessions.

Nelson had turned down a request to write arrangements for Paul McCartney but did write an arrangement of George Harrison's "Something" for Frank Sinatra. His stunning string arrangement was originally commissioned by Sinatra for a special concert he performed with the L.A. Philharmonic Orchestra on November 10th, 1974, at the Dorothy Chandler Pavilion in Los Angeles. A 107-piece orchestra under the direction of Zubin Mehta accompanied Sinatra for this special performance. However, Sinatra wouldn't actually record "Something" until 1979 for his *Trilogy* album.

Sadly, the Sinatra/Riddle collaboration was to come to a sudden end after 25 glorious years. Their special relationship will be remembered for producing timeless musical magic that is forever enshrined in the annals of American popular music.

Christopher Riddle explains: "Sinatra and my father had their schism around 1977/78. There was the Peter Meremblum Junior Symphony Orchestra. My father had been very active in fundraising for the orchestra. In fact, I used to spend most of my Saturdays helping him. In light of this, they decided to give a Nelson Riddle tribute dinner at the Century Plaza Hotel, and they asked Frank if he would be the compere. He said he would be delighted and everything but that's not how it panned out as they constantly moved the date, four times in total, to accommodate Frank's schedule. In the end, he sent his lawyer, Micky Rudin, in his stead. My father was heartbroken and said, 'I will never work for that man again.' Gregory Peck was involved in helping re-organise the event and did a great deal of work in getting people to come in and take up the slack, so to speak. I think my father and Gregory Peck became rather friendly thereafter. We did the 50th anniversary of the Oscars in 1978, and it was just natural he would have my father at the party, post ceremony.

Frank Sinatra and Christopher Riddle at Frank's first "retirement" party. Photograph courtesy Christopher Riddle personal collection.

```
"ALL STAR PARTY FOR FRANK SINATRA" -
REHEARSAL AND TAPING SCHEDULE (CONT'D)


SATURDAY, 11/19/83 (CONT'D)


INDIVIDUAL CALLS:
(ON STAGE, READY TO GO)

  10:00A          STAND-INS
                  HUGH McPHILLIPS
                  JOHN LISBON WOOD

  2:00P           MONTY HALL

  3:00P           JAMES STEWART

  3:30P           CAROL BURNETT

  4:00P           RICHARD BURTON

  4:30P           TOMMY LASORDA

  4:45P           NELSON RIDDLE

  6:00P           ORCHESTRA

  6:30P           MICHELE LEE

                  EARL BROWN

  7:15P           FRANK SINATRA

  7:30P           VIC DAMONE
                  STEVE LAWRENCE

  9:00P           FOSTER BROOKS (APPROX.)
```

Revised rehearsal schedule for Sinatra All Star TV tribute 1983.
Photograph courtesy of The Nelson Riddle Memorial
Library at Arizona State University.

Sinatra had ended taking up a paying job in Miami, I think; in any case, he sent his lawyer Micky Rudin from Beverly Hills who looked like he was out of central casting for the Godfather movie. My father was totally distraught. I'll never forget him sitting on the stage afterwards. He had this big, crystal bowl with his name carved on it. He just sat there glumly, almost thinking, 'What you mean, there's no Santa Claus, there's no Father Christmas?' That's the way it was. That was the break-up."

Yet when it was all said and done, Sinatra decided the Riddle era, as great as it had been, was history. "There is no particular story, and if there is one, I don't know it," Riddle told the NPR interviewer Robert Windeler not long before his death, at age 64, in 1985. "Sinatra is not inhibited by any particular loyalty. He had to think of Frank. I was hurt by it, I felt bad, but I think I was dimly aware that nothing is forever. A different wave of music had come in, and I was closely associated with him in a certain [other] type of music, so he moved into other areas. It's almost like one changes one's clothes. I saw him do it with Axel Stordahl; I should have realized that it would be my turn. He just moved on."

Christopher Riddle: "Dad and Frank never really worked again until Dec 1984, when Frank called from Washington DC, and Frank asked him if he wanted to do what they did for Kennedy in 1961, for the Reagan inaugural in January 1985. My father saw that as an ideal opportunity to bury the hatchet. Prelude to that earlier in 1984, we did a big tribute fundraiser for the American Ballet Theatre at the Beverly Wilshire Hotel, Beverly Hills. Linda Ronstadt was there singing. We had a 55-piece orchestra, and she came out on stage looking down, and she saw Frank in the front row and said tongue-in-cheek, 'I hear you've been singing some of my songs!' Don't tell me that didn't have something to do with Frank re-connecting with Dad. Maybe he thought, 'I want my arranger back?' The penny dropped with Frank that maybe this is perfect timing to get back with Nelson."

Peter Asher, Linda Ronstadt's manager: "Nelson spoke of Sinatra in mixed terms. He would describe his genius but also talk about his incredible unpleasantness and clearly both were part of the equation. He would also mention his incredible loyalty."

In 1983, around the time Nelson was working with Linda Ronstadt, there was a televised *All-Star Party for*

Frank Sinatra. The host was movie icon James Stewart. Nelson was musical director. The audience was a veritable who's who of film and television. Panning around and across the tables were "hot" TV stars of the time such as Mike Connors of *Mannix* fame and Daniel J. Travanti (*Hill Street Blues*) who I might say looked a little disinterested in the proceedings. Julio Iglesias performed the Latin version of "Begin the Beguine". There was Eydie Gormé looking on expectedly as her husband, Steve Lawrence, was due to perform. The world of stage and screen was represented by the likes of the Welsh screen superstar Richard Burton who was one of many guest presenters for the evening. Sitting in the centre-piece table was Frank Sinatra with wife Barbara.

A frail-looking Nelson introduced a vocal tribute to Sinatra which was performed by "two people you love and who love you", Steve Lawrence and Vic Damone. Nelson explained he had arranged an A-to-Z medley of Sinatra's songs.

A nervous yet grinning Steve Lawrence took the first number before passing the baton on and introducing Vic Damone. Belting out Nelson's sublimely arranged medley, the two veteran singers captivated their audience including "Ole Blue Eyes" himself who joined in with the final chorus of "Zing Went The Strings of My Heart".

"**A**ll or Nothing At All" (Lawrence), "**B***ewitched, Bothered and Bewildered*" (Damone), "**C**ome Fly With Me" (Lawrence), "**D**ay in, Day Out" (Lawrence and Damone), "**E**mbraceable You" (Damone), "**F**oggy Day" (Lawrence), "**G**et Happy" (Lawrence and Damone), "**H**ere's that Rainy Day" (Damone), "**I**'ll Never Smile

Again" (Lawrence), "**J**ust One of Those Things", "A **K**iss Goodnight", "**L**ady Is a Tramp" (Lawrence and Damone), "**M**y Kind of Town", "**N**ew York, New York" (Lawrence and Damone), "**O**h, Look at Me Now" (Damone), "**P**ut Your Dreams Away" (Lawrence), "**Q**uiet Nights, Quiet Stars" (Damone), "**R**ing a Ding Ding" (Lawrence and Damone), "**S**trangers in the Night" (Lawrence), "**T**his Love of Mine" (Damone), "**U**nder a Blanket of Blue" (Lawrence), "**V**iolets for Your Furs" (Damone), "**W**hen You're Smiling" (Lawrence and Damone), "E**X**actly like You, **Y**oung At Heart" (Lawrence and Damone), "**Z**ing Went the Strings of Your Heart" (Lawrence, Damone, and Sinatra).

CBS reviewed thus:

"Hosted by James Stewart, this TV special celebrated the long career of Frank Sinatra. First, Carol Burnett declares that she is "the original bobby-soxer" and describes her early memories of attending a concert of Sinatra's in New York City. Sinatra introduced his family members, including wife, Barbara Marx. Dionne Warwick and Michele Lee (Knots Landing) took the stage to perform a medley of Sinatra's songs, including 'Don't Fence Me In', 'Don't Get Around Much Anymore', 'I'll Walk Alone', 'I'll Be Seeing You', 'Long Ago and Far Away', 'People Will Say We're in Love', 'Nature Boy', 'Now is the Hour', 'The Trolley Song' and others.

"Ricardo Montalban introduced Julio Iglesias, who performed 'Volver a Empezar', a Spanish-language version of 'Begin the Beguine'.

"Actor Richard Burton then discussed the generosity of 'Mr. Anonymous', describing Sinatra as a 'street-corner poet', and Sinatra was visibly moved by his friend's words. Monty Hall, president of Variety Clubs International, talked about the foundation's charitable events, explaining how various children's hospital wings have been donated in the names of the previous honourees. Cary Grant read out a personal statement from President Reagan, complimenting Sinatra on the honour, and Hall explained that a new Frank Sinatra wing will be constructed at a Seattle Children's Hospital. Sinatra took the stage and thanked his many friends, requesting that the wing be named in honour of his entire family, rather than just himself. Burnett then noted that the following day was Sinatra's 68th birthday, and all of the guests serenaded him with 'Happy Birthday to You'."

The following year, Quincy Jones was putting an album together with Sinatra. Jones approached Nelson to write a couple of arrangements for an album titled *LA is My Lady,* but true to form, Nelson advised Jones that he would only arrange a full album. It was originally intended that Sinatra would duet with Lena Horne, but there was a delay as she had voice issues. Sinatra couldn't wait for her as he had other longstanding engagements. As a result, Sinatra revisited the project but just as a solo album. It was to be his final album as a solo artist. It was released in August 1984. Six different arrangers were used. Jones arranged the title track which he also part composed.

Nelson's long time bass trombone player and copyist, Terry Woodson, recalls, "By 1985, am not sure Frank and he had quite buried the hatchet, but when Nelson's health was failing, Frank was one of the first to call him at the hospital and promised him the next album. I think he was trying to offer Nelson some encouragement. Sadly, Nelson passed shortly thereafter."

(27)   60.

"THE DEFINITIVE SINATRA"   "THE DEFINITIVE SINATRA"
(Richard Burton)

(RICHARD BURTON RISES ON
APPLAUSE FROM MEDLEY)

                                        (APPLAUSE)

            RICHARD BURTON (BOOM) (AREA: B
                                    TABLE: 22)
I have never sung a song with

Frank Sinatra. Never acted with

him, shared his stage nor been a

member of an orchestra under his

baton. Nor was I privileged to

present either of his Oscars, his

Emmy, nor even one of his nine

Grammys on those memorable occasions.

I have, however, risen to my feet

to applaud his artistry, which is

without horizon, at numerous charity

performances raising mountains of

millions for the victims of the world.

I do know the rules of tonight:

this is a party for him as Friend,

not a Tribute to him as Humanitarian

(at his own insistence, I might add).

But I am compelled to say out loud,

here and now, what a lot of us have

been whispering for years, fully

aware it is what he likes to hear

least, and discourages most.

            (MORE)

65

(27)   61.

                    RICHARD BURTON (CONT'D)
You are a giant, Frank Sinatra.
Among the givers of the world, you
stand tallest. You have more than
paid rent for the space you occupy
on this planet, forged as you are
from legendary loyalty and compassion
concealed... concealed because you
have ordered it to be thus. Other
than yourself, there is no possessor
of the fullness of your generosity.
You have chosen to be the sole
keeper of that flame...
Mr. Anonymous you have asked to be;
Mr. Anonymous you shall be called.
At the risk of further offending you,
I appear as the herald of grateful
multitudes who have opened those
unexpected envelopes, special
delivering answers to their prayers...
those awakened by late night phone
calls which remedied their problems
only on condition they share your
covenant of secrecy... those who
were surprised by signed checks with
amounts not filled in...
                    (MORE)

Richard Burton tribute to Frank Sinatra All Star TV party 1983. Courtesy
of The Nelson Riddle Memorial Library Arizona State University.

5. WITHOUT A SONG

Without a song the day would never end
Without a song the road will never bend

Nelson was essentially Capitol Records' music director for a period of eleven years from 1951 to 1962. Naturally, a lot of his time was spent in the recording studio or as Nelson described it, "That wonderful, mysterious, acoustically sensitive cave." This was his golden period: working with Nat Cole, Peggy Lee, Dean Martin, Keely Smith, Judy Garland, Ella Fitzgerald, Johnny Mathis and many other top notch artists. It was during this time that he was introduced to Frank Sinatra. The rest, as the old adage goes, is history.

As an artist in his own right, he managed to fit in the recording of many instrumental albums and singles, one being "Lisbon Antigua", a huge hit and million-selling gold record. This tune was also used in a feature film, an espionage thriller called *Lisbon* starring Ray Milland.

When it came to vocalists, Nelson acknowledged early on that each singer's musical capabilities and egos were different. For example, he contrasted the easy going laid-back demeanour of Nat Cole with that of a more feisty, pro-active approach by Frank Sinatra. Cole had no knowledge of classical music and preferred a simple jazz feel. Sinatra, on the other hand, couldn't read music but was fascinated by the classical composers. This close alignment with Nelson's own study meant a meeting of minds and enabled Nelson to use more expressive openings.

I spoke with Chris Walden, big band arranger for Michael Bublé: "Nelson's arrangements are so rich in sound and orchestrations, he likes to fill a hole where the singer would come in, but amazingly, he never steps on the singer. He never overwrites. On many of his arrangements, you can remove the vocals and they would stand alone with their own meaning as an instrumental, as the counterpoint Nelson makes is almost a tune in itself. That said, once you put the vocal in even with the counterpoint, it doesn't infringe on the singer."

Nelson created a sound which is unique and easy to identify, even for non-musicians. I would describe it as being subtle, definitely commercial but tailored. By tailored I mean he wrote specifically with the artist in mind. He viewed the voice as another instrument in the orchestra. He would write intriguing introductions and endings; those were his signatures. The rest of his arrangements were designed with the singer in mind, to create space and orchestral backings that brought out the best in the performer."

Christopher Riddle: "What makes Dad's sound so special is its simplicity—less is more. He will start with one section of the orchestra, then hand off to another section, and so on, then he brings them all together. Then there's a diminuendo, and it's all over."

A classic example of this is a number 3 hit record, "The Blacksmith Blues" by Ella Mae-Morse. Fellow arranger Billy May was extremely busy; it was December 1951. He gave Nelson an early Christmas present by offering the chance for Nelson to do an arrangement for the young singer, a 78rpm single. "The Blacksmith Blues" was the result. Nelson had to create a new arrangement from an old magnetic tape originally intended for Ella Fitzgerald. He introduced a sound where the tapping of a glass ashtray (well, several, as they tended to break) was used to create the sound of a Blacksmith's anvil. The crescendo of various instruments gives an early insight into the Nelson Riddle sound. A jazzy, uplifting, swinger of a number, it was a big hit for the singer and a statement piece from the arranger. The success of this recording provided further evidence to Capitol that they were right to employ the young arranger on a full-time basis. If you happen by this record, please take time to listen to it.

Nelson is mostly associated with the success of the albums he did with Frank Sinatra and perhaps rightly so, but such is the range and diverse nature of his work there should be special mention of other collaborations with other notable male and female vocalists.

Aside from his work with Sinatra and Nat Cole, the latter being previously well documented, where should I start? I will endeavour to cover it in chronological fashion as time can reveal other contributing factors to the mood of the music, as well as some social commentary on the period in question. My choices do not cover every collaboration that Nelson entered into, some have been excluded, not from a critical standpoint but from a subjective point of view. Many other significant recordings are covered in a different chapter.

My musings are in the main about album collaborations although single hits may have emanated from the album release. Instrumental album or single releases comprising of tunes rather than songs may seem to contradict the title of this chapter, but I believe the semantics to be the same.

Keely Smith recording session. Photograph courtesy of
Christopher Riddle's personal collection.

Nelson's first album collaboration with Judy Garland.
Photograph Capitol Records. Cover design Bob Willoughby.

Nelson combined with Billy Eckstine to complete the
MGM release "Kiss of Fire". An early Nelson example,
but you still recognise the Riddle sound developing
with the bright dominant opening. The song reached
number 16 on the Billboard charts, although the tune is

probably more well known as an instrumental. This version by Eckstine released on 1st January 1953 is very melodic, and he gives a fine performance dealing with lyrics that many lesser vocalists would struggle to convey. Eckstine's dulcet tones are legendary although in career terms he suffered a backlash after being photographed in an intimate pose with a white woman resting her head on his shoulder. This did not go down well with the record buying public who were predominantly white and not ready to see a black man with a white woman in such close proximity.

Therefore, although Eckstine was greatly revered by his peers, he didn't get the commercial return his talent deserved. His distinctive, rich baritone voice is evident on a duet he did with Sarah Vaughan for a song called "Passing Strangers" which was a minor hit in 1965. It may not have reached the heights in terms of chart success but has commanded iconic status as one of the most instantly recognisable duets in post war popular music.

Another single release for Nelson around that time was "No Matter How You Say Goodbye" by Betty Hutton. Released on Capitol in 1953, it was the B side of "Goin' Steady", which was the swingiest of the two, and the one which charted, reaching number 21. Hutton was well known for her film and stage career, playing Annie Oakley in *Annie Get Your Gun (1950)*. She was active from the late 30's right through to the early 1980's. She married Capitol executive Alan J. Livingston in 1955, but they divorced five years later.

The year of Elvis Presley's television debut, 1955, was slam bang in the middle of his work with Sinatra, yet workaholic Nelson was still able to compose an instrumental album for Capitol titled *The Music from*

Oklahoma. This album warrants a mention not least because Nelson had not seen or heard any music from the successful Broadway show or the movie starring Gordon Macrae and Shirley Jones. He orchestrated the entire album on his own account. He would go on to comment modestly that was the reason the tunes bore no resemblance to previous renditions. Modestly is the operative word here because he was subsequently contacted by Richard Rodgers who had written the music. Rodgers was absolutely blown away by Nelson's innovative and original interpretations. So much so he told him he had wished Nelson had scored the movie!

Judy is an album with Judy Garland released in 1956, the year *My Fair Lady* opened on Broadway. Nelson's arrangements for *Judy* sees him get the best out of Garland especially on the opening track, the Harold Arlen composition, the memorable "Come Rain or Come Shine". This was Nelson's favourite arrangement on this album as it highlighted Garland's unique vibrato voice. Nelson was attracted to her voice and completed twenty or so arrangements for her spread over two albums. A musical marriage of singer and arranger, they complement each other. The vulnerability in her voice is typical Garland, her musical crutch is Nelson Riddle. The album artwork includes a photograph by famed American photographer Bob Willoughby.

Nelson, busy as he was, still had time to squeeze in an instrumental hit of his own, "Port Au Prince", which reached number 21 on the charts. It's a tune that one readily recognises yet maybe the title doesn't sit in the memory. Nelson gives it the full orchestral treatment.

The following year came Nelson's first collaboration with Peggy Lee. The album titled *The Man I Love*, arrangements by Riddle, conducted by Sinatra! This release was described by critic William Ruhlmann as "a superb pairing of singer, conductor and arranger". Track no.12 became the now definitive version of the iconic suburban composition by Oscar Hammerstein and Jerome Kern "The Folks Who Live on The Hill".

A highly regarded debut album by Keely Smith, *I Wish You Love,* followed. Nelson's opening is reminiscent of an introduction to a movie. Smith's vocals are well supported by backing singers, and the song, a ballad, is un-mistakably given the Riddle treatment, maintaining its romantic theme, whilst given a slight up-tempo boost. Music with a heartbeat.

Capitol also released a hit album of Nelson's instrumentals called *C'mon Get Happy* which made the top twenty of the Billboard Easy Listening charts. The tracks included the title tune "Get Happy" and the melodic, easy on the ear "Time Was", a Miguel Prado and S.K. Russell composition.

In 1958, the 30th Academy Awards saw *The Bridge on the River Kwai* win 7 Oscars including Best Picture. Nelson as part of an "Exotica" trend released *Sea of Dreams.*

Ambient Exotica's partial review is as follows: "Nelson himself was his biggest competitor in the realms of string-laden Easy Listening. His own album, *C'mon... Get Happy*, released in the same year, was a more successful album, peaking at number 20 in the Billboard Charts. However, *Sea of Dreams* is much more lush, romantic and, most important in the given context, exotic. If you are craving for the romantic side of the Exotica genre, you are making the right choice with *Sea of Dreams*. Instead of interweaving exotic percussion with the surroundings, Riddle concentrates exclusively on the strings, leaving a small niche for mallet instruments and bells of all kinds.

"In his later years, Riddle presented some variety in his albums, but here, the sphere of action is much more restricted, or as the saying goes, once you know one song, you know them all. The coherence isn't bad at all, though."

That year also saw Nelson write arrangements for another album with Judy Garland titled *Judy In Love*. Produced by Voyle Gilmore at Capitol, once again Nelson's opening arrangement, in this case "Zing Went the Strings of My Heart", captures the best of Garland's vocals shining a light on her unique timbre and inflections.

Christopher Riddle: "I remember as a young boy Judy visiting our house. She was wearing a plaster cast at the time. I recall she was very petite at that time. Dad loved working with Judy, and it was reciprocated. After she left, we noticed that some of the plaster cast had become stuck to the chair she had been sitting on. Mom said, 'Leave that be, don't sit on that chair!' Mind you, she was less enamoured when she saw the publicity still of Judy sitting on my dad's lap."

The same year, the first year of the Grammys saw Nelson's instrumental LP *Cross Country Suite,* featuring clarinettist Buddy De Franco. This album won the 1959 Grammy for Best Original Instrumental Composition. Described by Marc Myers as "pure ear candy", Nelson does indeed take us cross country. The up-tempo, busy "Metropolis" through the harmonically serene opening in "The Mississippi" then taking us up for a break in "Smoky Mountain Country". De Franco's marvellous clarinet solos are supported by a combination of soothing strings and muted brass.

Rosemary Acerra: "*Cross Country Suite* was important for Dad because it allowed him to explore the kind of composing he would do for movie scores, impressionistic and visual, music that painted a picture. It's been important to me because when it was recorded when I was 10 years old. I latched onto the sound of it, and it became an emotional attachment."

Nelson worked with jazz singer Sue Raney at Capitol when she was just seventeen years of age. He arranged her debut album, *When Your Lover Has Gone,* and was to work with her again in London for the BBC seven years later.

Christopher Riddle recalls it very well: "I had a huge crush on Sue Raney at the time. I was just fourteen years of age, and she would be nearly ten years older. I was just finding out what sexual attraction was all about. I remember we all stayed as the prestigious Mayfair Hotel in London's West End.

"I was work to with Sue forty-six years later when conducting the orchestra at Carnegie Hall, New York, when Patti La Belle was doing an Ella Fitzgerald tribute show. I was able to do some of Dad's instrumentals including the theme to TV show *Route 66* which was hit record for Dad, plus 'Metropolis' from his *Cross-Country Suite*. I was so happy to have a 72-piece orchestra at my disposal that day."

Sue remembers her time working with Nelson as if it were yesterday. I spoke to her at her home in Los Angeles:

"I went to audition for the Ray Anthony TV show back in 1956. The auditions were held in Santa Monica, California. I wasn't aware at the time, but Lee Gillette, the A and R guy at Capitol, was present. Lee was so nice and encouraged me although I didn't get signed that night. After that, I did an EP from the film *The Girl Can't Help It*. As a guest singer, my song was 'Every Time'. Although I was only 17 years old, Lee Gillette came back to me and said, 'We want to sign you.'

"On top of that, Nelson Riddle was to be my arranger. Imagine that. Nelson was warm and very considerate. My big song was 'When Your Lover Has Gone'. An EP followed on from that which was taken from the film *The Music Man*. I sang 'Till there was you'.

"In 1961, I was very proud to be invited to be a small part of the President Kennedy inauguration party. I travelled with Nelson, Frank Sinatra, and Peter Lawford. I was sitting at the back of the plane in awe, observing all these Hollywood stars. I sang at one of those inauguration balls. It was a great thrill and honour for me. Nelson made me feel so comfortable. I adored Nelson and got to work with him again on the Rosemary Clooney show as a guest star; that was also a wonderful experience.

"It was later when I came to London to record the TV show *The Best of Both Worlds* in 1965, when I met up with Nelson and his children Skip, Christopher, and Rosemary. I flew over to London, but Nelson and his family came over on the Queen Mary, which was only a four-day crossing at the time. Nelson was married to Doreen at the time, and she was in quite a fragile state. Nelson said, 'If you go to the ladies room together, please look after her.' Yvonne Littlewood was the BBC producer for that show. She was wonderful. Nelson was a workaholic and liked to do live dates. He would phone me and say we have a gig here and a gig there. I would be the girl singer for the band."

Dinah Shore, Yes Indeed! was a Capitol release from 1958. It includes tracks like "Sentimental Journey" and the title track "Yes Indeed", a Sy Oliver composition. Many reviewers rate it as their favourite Dinah Shore album.

"I've had this album for over 40 years, and it's never far from the turntable. I love the medleys and, of course, the Nelson Riddle production. Dinah was at her peak here, and her voice is just like warm honey."

Chileans experienced a change in their taste in music during the 1950s, when bolero music overtook tango as Chileans' preferred music genre. "Bolero" crops up again! Lucho Gatica was a Chilean superstar at the time known as the "King of Bolero", and so, in 1958, it was natural fit for Capitol to put Lucho with Nelson for "Mexicali Rose". Whilst not "Bolero" music in the true sense of the word, I can detect a little nod to Ravel in Nelson's underscore.

Sing a Song with Riddle was another ground-breaking instrumental album. Released in 1959, the year of the tragic death of Buddy Holly and Richie Valens, the album consists of arrangements for a vocalist but without a singer. Karaoke, I hear you say? Yes, but ground-breaking as karaoke was a few years away from being developed. This was a pioneering development by Nelson, well ahead of its time. The album received mixed reviews but maybe that was because the critics hadn't fully understood the rationale behind the recording. There are twelve tracks in total, many of the standards of American popular music. See if you can *Sing a Song with Riddle.*

The same year saw the Verve release *Ella Fitzgerald Sings The George and Ira Gershwin Songbook*. During the late '50s, Fitzgerald continued her "Songbook" records releasing a series of albums. This particular set featured 59 songs matching the year they were released—all written by George and Ira Gershwin. More accurately speaking, the albums consisted of 53 songs and 6 instrumentals, including "The Ambulatory Suite", allowing Nelson to draw on his experience of the French impressionists. This marathon production by Norman Grantz took over eight months to put together. "But Not For Me" won Fitzgerald the 1960 Grammy for Best Female Vocal Performance. Many respected critics rank this album among Fitzgerald's very best recordings. Their work together included three of her landmark "songbook" albums, devoted to George and Ira Gershwin, Jerome Kern and Johnny Mercer.

The 59 tune Gershwin box set with Ella.

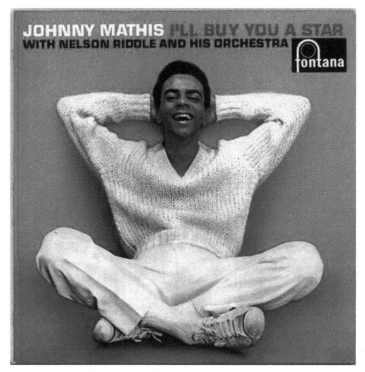

I'll Buy You a Star Johnny Mathis. Photograph Fontana Records.

Christopher Riddle: "I remember when Dad did the George and Ira Gershwin songbook with Ella. It was a compilation of five long playing records. I remember also there was a deluxe edition which came in a driftwood-coloured wooden case. Ella gave my father a Phillipe Patek watch when they'd finished it. It was inscribed 'to Nelson love Ella'. My father used to wear alligator watch bands (straps). This watch in 18ct gold was the thinnest in the world. It was a manual wind. He prized this watch but 'lost' it in New York many years later attending a discotheque with two of my younger sisters. He wouldn't pursue with the police although there wouldn't be any around with that inscription. If anyone has the watch and would like to return it to me, I would be very grateful. No awkward questions asked!

"We did an album with her in the late 70's called *Dream Dancing*. I was playing bass trombone. Dad was very fond of Ella, and the feeling was mutual. As a matter fact, I took my wife, Elizabeth, to visit Ella at her home in Whittier Drive in Beverly Hills, just off of Sunset Boulevard. She had a Spanish, Moorish style house. It was a beautiful place. She had a dark green Pullman Mercedes 600 limousine, which she was driven around in. She was upstairs in her bedroom watching TV quiz shows and soap operas, that's what she liked to do. We went upstairs to see her and next to her bed were photos of my father and our family—we were very close to her. Her son Ray Brown Jr., whose father was Ray Brown, was usually in attendance. The last time I saw Ella later on in life, she was in a wheelchair. She had to have both legs amputated due to circulation issues; terrible for her. She was never feeling sorry for herself or hard done-by. She was just Ella. She didn't live much longer after that. She never complained. She was really something."

For Johnny Mathis's *I'll Buy You a Star,* Nelson took temporary leave and jumped over to Columbia for this collaboration with Mathis. This album was to make the Billboard's magazines chart in May 1961. Once again, Nelson's orchestrations showcased the singer in the best possible light. Both arranger and singer excel on this album. Mathis's distinctive tenor gels perfectly with Nelson's arrangement. From a personal perspective, I like track no. 2, "Stairway to the Stars", especially how expertly Nelson creates space for Mathis's astronomical finish; this track is four minutes fifty seconds of magical, heavenly music.

Johnny Mathis gave me an exclusive statement about his time working with Nelson: "I had the pleasure of first meeting and working with Nelson when I was in my early 20's. We recorded 2 albums together for which I will always consider myself particularly fortunate.

Very few great arrangers and composers ever become a household name but along with the likes of Henry Mancini and Percy Faith, almost every family had several albums with Nelson's name on the cover.

Beyond his movie and television work, Nelson carved out a niche for himself as one of the primo arrangers in popular music, as is evidenced by the assortment of singers that sought out his talent for so many years. I am very proud to consider myself one of them."

In 1961, Nelson composed an instrumental album, *Love Tide*.

A detailed review by the website Ambient Exotica contrasted the album to Riddle's earlier water themed *Sea of Dreams* and wrote that, "The most glaring example for the different soundscapes between both albums are the instruments that are neglected on the first work, but added in the latter: vibraphones, harps, pianos and bongos altogether lessen the romantic notions in *Love Tide* but cannot leave an impact once the melodrama and yearning are aurally displayed via the many violin strings. ...And since Riddle occasionally breaks the overarching concept that is thrown at him by the marketing people at Capitol, you should not expect an adamant frame that solely focuses on the loving couple of the front cover, let alone the liquidous setting. That's actually great, for it is these formula-expanding moments where the album starts to get interesting for Exotica followers, regardless of whether they are fans of Nelson Riddle or not."

Shirley Bassey had numerous hits in the UK in the 1960's. Her collaboration with Nelson produced the album *Let's Face The Music* in 1962, and it reached No. 12 in the UK album chart; and the single, "What Now My Love?" made it to No. 5. Vic Lewis who was Nelson's "go-to" man in London brought Nelson over to England at the request of Norman Newell, Bassey's producer. The album was recorded on the EMI/Columbia label. The hit song "What Now My Love?" is now regarded as one of Bassey's signature tunes. Nelson's orchestration creates space for her voice to excel and the younger Bassey doesn't disappoint. It is interesting to note that "What Now, My Love?" is the English title of a popular song whose original French version, "Et maintenant?" was written in 1961 by composer Gilbert Bécaud and lyricist Pierre Delanoë.

The recurring musical pattern in the background is the "Bolero" by Ravel. English lyrics and the title were written by Carl Sigman. Once again, Nelson was re-united with Ravel's "Bolero" and through his continuous study of Ravel, he was able to optimize the level of his orchestration by his "less is more approach". The introduction and the ending is pure Ravel. The rest of the album is very well produced, and there are many favourites like "Let's Fall In Love" and the title track "Let's Face the Music and Dance". The album was re-packaged for release in the USA on United Artists but had different track listings and alternative recordings being titled *Shirley Bassey sings the Hit Songs from Oliver.*

The year 1962 was the time of the football (soccer) World Cup in Chile and the year of Bob Dylan's debut album. Nelson was to record his second album with Dean Martin, *Cha Cha de Amor*. The title is a bit of a give-away in terms of music genre. It was built around what was described as an "authentic Afro-Cuban rhythm section". One of the tracks, "For Sentimental Reasons", illustrates Nelson's versatility as an arranger. On this album, it swings nicely for Martin; contrast this to the arrangement for Ella Fitzgerald and later Linda Ronstadt. The same song yet delivered in entirely different ways, affirming Christopher Riddle's assertion that his father didn't do "cookie cutter" arrangements. They were always tailored to the individual singer.

This is more than illustrated by another album collaboration of Nelson's, *Country Boy* (1963) with Pinky Tomlin. A strange combination. The liner notes from the album give a better insight: "*Country Boy* is a collection of songs and top talent, bringing back that 'country boy' of all times, Pinky Tomlin. Here we have the timeless artistry of one of America's great vocalists, together with the magic of one of the country's top arrangers and conductors, Nelson Riddle. This is a wild combination. From their performance there has been achieved the unusual and the different, so necessary to recognition today. To Pinky Tomlin's old friends, this album will be most welcome; and for youngsters who haven't yet had the pleasure of hearing and enjoying Pinky, a new style and a new singing idol will have come along."

An instrumental release of note was the 1964 album on the Verve label simply called *Oscar Peterson and Nelson Riddle*. The award-winning Canadian jazz pianist teamed up with Nelson, and the result is what you would expect when two maestros work together. Andrew Cartmel of London Jazz news views the album as significant and one of the most under-rated in either Riddle's or Peterson's catalogue.

Another significant album was released the following year, this time with Jack Jones on the Kapp label. Jones was at the peak of his powers at the time and the album

There's Love and There's Love and There's Love which, according to Jason Ankeny of AllMusic, "pairs the singer with the immortal arranger Nelson Riddle for a dizzyingly romantic collection of ballads as light and gentle as summer rain." I did contact Jack Jones and left a couple of voicemails asking for his memories of working with Nelson, but he declined to comment.

The "Father of Bossa Nova", Antonio Carlos Jobim, was Nelson's next collaborator. The label was Warner Bros and the producer Jimmy Hilliard, The album with a Latin jazz and bossa nova feel had the grand title, *The Wonderful World of Antonio Carlos Jobim*. Peter Levinson in his book, *September in the Rain*, regarded this album as the most beautiful album Nelson ever arranged. Personally, I wouldn't go that far, but it is a nice album and ranks highly in the plethora of music partnerships Nelson entered into.

Christopher Riddle: "When my father did that 1965 album with Carlos Albert Jobim, he stayed with us for a couple of weeks at our house, 3853 Carbon Canyon Road, in Malibu. After we had dinner, he would play for us, can you imagine?

"Dad worked with everyone at Capitol. That's one reason why he was happy to go over with Frank to Reprise in 1964. He said he felt he had become akin to a piece of the furniture at Capitol. They put him with everyone from Georgia Carr through Dinah Shore to Al Martino."

Eddie Fisher was backed by Nelson on the RCA Victor label for the album *Games That Lovers Play*. It was a 1966 release, the year the England soccer team finally won the FIFA World Cup. The title song was initially released as a single, and Fisher had his first chart entry for over five years. It reached no. 2 in the Billboard easy listening charts. Fisher's record deal with Dot Records had expired and off the back of the single's success of *Games That Lovers Play,* RCA Victor quickly signed Fisher. The album followed with Nelson providing arrangements to showcase Fisher's deeper delivery allowing the singer to be more expressive in his interpretation.

One singer who was signed to Capitol at a later date was Vic Damone, considered by Sinatra to have "the best pipes in the business". Nelson did, however, do two or three recordings with Damone for a compilation album. "Desafinado", is a Antonio Carlos Jobim composition which unsurprisingly has a nice, smooth Latin feel to it. There is a long intro from Nelson which sets the scene perfectly. There was also "Games That Lovers Play" which had been recorded previously by Eddie Fisher, amongst others. Damone is singing on more familiar territory on that one as it is a ballad; however, Nelson's orchestration helps the song build the tempo getting the best out of Damone vocals. Finally, there is the song from the film *Black Orpheus* titled "The Day in The Life of a Fool" aka "Carnival (Manha de Carnaval)". Here Nelson's opening is very distinctive and resonates throughout the song which is beautifully delivered by Damone. It was a shame Nelson hadn't recorded a full album with Vic Damone as it is widely believed that Nelson would have brought the best out of Damone's vocal instrument.

In the early 2000's, I got to work with Perry Damone, Vic's son, and was able to assist on an album production for Vic's signature label. I also got to meet and interview him for a music magazine publication. We spoke off record about Nelson's work with Sinatra, Vic's idol. He regretted not working more with Nelson but was supportive of son Christopher's effort to keep the Nelson Riddle Orchestra on the road; indeed, Christopher had provided backing for Vic Damone and Diahann Carroll when they were touring their double act as husband and wife back in the early 90's.

Vic Damone and Diahann Carroll. Christopher Riddle backed them when they were touring as a double act. Photograph courtesy Perry Damone's personal collection.

In 1967, Nelson brought the family over to London, England, for a TV show he was doing with singer Matt Monro. It was titled *Matt Monro meets Nelson Riddle*. Gillian Lynne was the choreographer for the show, and it was once again produced by Yvonne Littlewood. The show was live and recorded for an album release by EMI called *Matt Sings Nelson Swings* which includes a number of Monro's hits like "Born Free" and "Softly As I Leave You", plus Nelson's arrangement for Monro's vocal on "Strike Up The Band." There is also conversation between the pair as Nelson introduced his instrumental, the "John F Kennedy March".

Nelson's switch to Reprise wasn't wholly successful, partly due to Sinatra selling a controlling share to Warner Bros, but it was intertwined with a massive shift in music tastes. The standards were perceived as old-fashioned music in an era of the swinging sixties and rock and roll. In the late sixties and during the seventies, Nelson's work shifted from writing orchestrations for vocalists to concentrate on film scores, TV series and televised variety shows.

6. LET'S GO TO THE MOVIES

Bette Davis is probably lying,
and Greta Garbo is probably crying.

The opening of a song is one of the opportunities where the arranger can make a statement. *Let's Go To The Movies* from the musical *Annie* is not a Nelson Riddle arrangement, but I think Nelson would approve. The arrangement is by Ralph Burns, a lesser-known contemporary of Nelson.

When drawing up a budget for a prospective movie project, an indie film producer will work together with a line producer to establish a line-by-line breakdown of estimated costs. These are divided into two sections, above the line costs and below the line costs. This principle will apply to the big studio accountants when determining their big buck blockbusters.

Above the line costs will include the salaries of the main cast and the writers and director's fees. Below the line costs have a plethora of various skills essential to the making of a successful movie, most of the crew carry out their duties during the filming process. As regards the music department, their contribution is normally made in the post-production process.

A good producer and his director will recognise the importance of having a great musical score that will help convey and enhance the storytelling. There are many examples of this, and a number of directors have their favoured composers such as Hitchcock/ Hermann, Spielberg/Williams, etc. Although the music compositions may be finalised after the film footage has been produced, discussions may have taken place much earlier in the film production process. The director will share his vision with his music man and hope for a meeting of minds resulting in an outstanding and memorable score. How many of us remember our favourite movie scores? If you were to list your own favourites, what would they be?

Nelson Riddle's film work is plentiful and perhaps understated, but not anymore! I have covered most of the Sinatra and clan-associated movies in a previous chapter, but there were many other film credits.

As far as the records determine, Nelson's first film assignment was in 1953. Commissioned by director Richard Quine at Columbia, he was to write arrangements for *All Ashore,* a Mickey Rooney vehicle, which was a take-off of *On The Town*, where three sailors finally get shore leave and go in search of fun and girls!

Later that year, *The Blue Gardenia* was released. Directed by the legendary Fritz Lang, it had Nelson arranging the title tune. This was later recorded by Nat "King" Cole who actually performed it as a lounge singer in the movie. The film starred Anne Baxter and Richard Conte, who was one of the four in the successful TV series in the 1960's called *The Four Just Men.*

After working with Frederick Hollander for Stanley Kramer's *The 5,000 Fingers of Dr. T.,* Nelson was assigned to write some arrangements for Dimitri Tiomkin for a 1954 release titled *The Adventures of Hajji Baba,* a Persian fantasy adventure which had the enigmatic John Derek in the lead role.

The following year, Nelson extended his now formidable experience of film composition by being an orchestrator for Alfred Newman in the Twentieth Century Fox production of *Carousel*, the famous musical fantasy about a fairground barker returning to Earth for one day—fifteen years after his death. It starred Gordon McRae as Billy Bigelow and Shirley Jones as Julie Jordan. There were many marvellous tunes, of course, by Rodgers and Hammerstein including "Soliloquy", an eight-minute solo, which was also recorded by Frank Sinatra. Then there is "You'll Never Walk Alone" which has become a global sporting anthem. I am not sure who adopted it first but Liverpool F.C. in the UK would no doubt be one that springs to mind.

Flame of the Islands for Republic Pictures was also made that year, shot on location in the Bahamas. It had Yvonne De Carlo in the lead role of Rosalind, alongside co-stars Zachary Scott, Howard Duff and James Arness (who would go on to play Marshall Matt Dillon in the hit TV western series *Gunsmoke)*. This a film noir melodrama about a café singer (Rosalind) who buys into a gambling casino, and the men who fall in love with her. Yvonne De Carlo was a singer in her own right, and she recorded a single release from *Flame of The Islands*. It appears that it was only a "promo" recorded by Capitol, not actually a commercial release. However, the song can be heard online, titled "Take or Leave It". The label gives equal billing for Nelson. It is a catchy little number which has a Goombay style beat, reflecting some of the Bahamian music culture.

Although not directly involved in the film production, *The Proud Ones,* a Twentieth Century Fox production in 1956, was to provide Nelson with a hit record, charting at no. 39. This western movie starred Robert Ryan as Marshal Cass Silver. His attempts to maintain law and order in a town full of unruly cowboys and a corrupt saloon owner are exacerbated by a sudden, intermittent loss of vision. Casting the lead role was almost a drama in itself. First it was Victor Mature, then later on Gregory Peck was set to star. Peck had other ideas and then in November 1955, it was announced that Gary Cooper would take the lead, but by late December, it was Robert Stack! Whatever the reason, Robert Ryan, fifth choice or not, did an excellent job. As so often happens, I cannot imagine any other actor playing the part so effectively. For western lovers, there is an iconic scene where Ryan's character teaches "Thad" the art of shooting, lawman style. The cinematography is a great shoot in more ways than one! Ryan was ably supported by Jeffrey Hunter as "Thad" and Virginia Mayo as "Sally", Ryan's soon to be fiancée. Robert Middleton play a "good baddie" (now there's an oxymoron if ever there was) as Honest John Barrett. The movie's theme which would garner that top 40 Billboard hit for Nelson is unique in that it has a haunting, whistling score throughout.

The year 1957 saw Nelson score the film musical *Pajama Game* starring Doris Day and John Raitt. It's about a pyjama factory worker who falls in love with a factory superintendent who has been hired by the boss to help oppose the workers' demand for a pay rise.

The original soundtrack album released by Columbia Records hit the top ten of the Billboard charts in 1957. John Raitt was among ten others who were in the original Broadway cast. Frank Sinatra was first choice to play superintendent Sid but he turned down the role so Warners reverted back to John Raitt to reprise the role from the stage version. This was to be his only lead role in films. Critics, whilst praising his incomparable high register baritone, panned his wooden acting and complete lack of any screen presence, despite an impressive and muscular physique. Director Bob Fosse was also retained as the film's choreographer. Doris Day admitted her role was very challenging as she tried to fit in with the majority of a cast who had played over a thousand performances on Broadway. She likened it to trying to find her place in a well-oiled machine.

The Girl Most Likely was the last movie to be shot at the RKO Hollywood Studio in Gower Street. The film had sat on the shelf for over a year until Universal gained the distribution rights. Jane Powell starred opposite Cliff Robertson. Powell was to comment that Universal didn't release the film; rather, they let it escape! Nelson wrote the score but was uncredited. I wouldn't think he was too concerned at the time. Despite the film's relative obscurity, the title song, a catchy little number, was composed by Nelson and was sung by the Hi-Lo's over the opening credits. Producer Stanley Rubin described the film as an orphan: RKO, the father, had died, and Universal, the mother, was in a coma, so the little girl had to look after herself.

Danny Kaye was a very popular comedy star and all-round entertainer in movies, TV, and theatres. He played an English schoolteacher in *Merry Andrew* which was released in 1958. Kaye's co-star was Pier Angeli, mother of my good friend, the late Perry Damone. The story sees Kaye, a creative yet downtrodden teacher, discover the joys of the travelling circus. Whilst on an archaeological trip, he meets circus acrobat Pier Angeli (who played in a high wire act in the *Story of Three Loves*), and they eventually fall in love. Despite the circus background, it isn't quite the madcap offering we usually expect from Kaye, more of a gentle rom-com. The composers were Saul Chaplin and Nelson Riddle, although Nelson is uncredited in that category. The Nelson Riddle sound is evident nonetheless in his conductorship and the oddly worded title of music adaptor. The latter probably means he did all the arrangements but wasn't credited as such, but that's only my opinion. It is strange but true that Nelson was nominated for the Golden Laurel as top Music Director for this movie; that was the film's only nomination.

L'il Abner is a musical comedy released in 1959. It is based on the comic strip of the same name created by Al Capp. The film was directed by Melvin Frank—starring Peter Palmer, Leslie Parrish, Billy Hayes and Stubby Kaye with supporting roles from Julie Newmar and Stella Stevens. Nelson shared composer responsibilities with Joseph J. Lilley on this one. Nelson was nominated for a Grammy Award for best soundtrack as well as receiving an Oscar nomination for best music scoring of a musical picture, only to lose out to André Previn who won for *Porgy and Bess*.

Lolita. Photograph Metro-Goldwyn-Mayer.

Paris When It Sizzles starring Audrey Hepburn and William Holden.
Photograph courtesy of Paramount Pictures.

What a Way To Go! A stellar cast. Photograph Twentieth Century Fox.

President Kennedy, Peter Sellers and Prime Minister Harold McMillan attend the film premiere of *Lolita* in London, England 1962. Photograph courtesy Paramount Pictures.

In May of 1962, Nelson was in London, England, to score *Lolita,* a Stanley Kubrick directed movie described in IMDb as "a middle-aged college professor becoming infatuated with a fourteen-year-old nymphet". It is an extremely controversial movie given the subject matter of Vladimir Nabokov's screenplay which is loosely based on his best-selling book of the same name. Kubrick made substantial changes to Nabokov's screenplay, mainly with the film censor in mind, yet Nabokov retained the screen credit. Kubrick's first choice as composer was Bernard Herrmann, but he turned it down as he didn't wish to use Bob Harris's "Theme from Lolita" in his score. Sue Lyon who played the title role did not attend the film premiere in New York as she was too young to see the film. She was, however, allowed to see the film in London later in the year.

Nelson composed the music (the main theme was by Bob Harris). The recurring dance number first heard on the radio when Humbert meets Lolita in the garden, later became a hit single under the name "Lolita Ya Ya" which turned out to be a hit single for Sue Lyon. A soundtrack review by an un-known source said, "The highlight is the most frivolous track, 'Lolita Ya Ya', a maddeningly vapid and catchy instrumental with nonsense vocals that comes across as a simultaneously vicious and good-humoured parody of the kitschiest elements of early-sixties rock and roll." Perhaps this was Nelson trying to get "his own back" with a dig at rock music which he continued to detest and blame for a downturn in his own career.

In 1964, Paramount Pictures released *Paris When It Sizzles,* a rom-com starring screen icons William Holden and Audrey Hepburn. This big budget (four million US dollars) film received mixed reviews. Nelson's score included "That Face Music" by Bergman/Spence and Nelson's arrangement of "The Girl Who Stole The Eiffel Tower" sung by Frank Sinatra.

The same year saw *What a Way To Go,* a big budget black comedy with a stellar cast of Shirley MacLaine, Paul Newman, Robert Mitchum, Dean Martin, Bob (Robert) Cummings and Dick Van Dyke. The director was J. Lee Thompson (known for *The Guns of Navarone*). Nelson's score includes the delightful "Louisa's Theme" as well as "Fabulous Penthouse" and "Get Acquainted".

Christopher Riddle: "Dad was working in London doing a lot of TV stuff at the time, and we were all invited to the film's premiere and afterwards at Claridges where there was a gala ball and dinner. My brother Skip, who was seventeen at the time, got to dance with Shirley MacLaine!

"Sitting at our table were two people called Lord and Lady Christopher Mann. They were the caretakers for Winston Churchill's home, Chartwell. They invited us to lunch there and gave us a private tour. We had a designated driver, Phantom Five Rolls Royce in Moss Green, who drove us all over the country."

Harlow, a biopic of screen legend Jean Harlow, was released in 1965 by Magna Films. It was a low budget affair filmed in black and white electrono-vision, a photographic technique which was later found to be largely unsuccessful for the big screen. Carol Lynley played the lead role supported by Efrem Zimbalist Jr. as William Mansfield. Ginger Rogers played Mama Jean. This was to be her last film before retiring in 1987. There was also a cameo role for former heavyweight champion of the world Sonny Liston. Nelson shared orchestration duties with Al Ham. The overture in this movie is a dramatic opus, over five minutes long.

The comedy *Marriage on the Rocks* was released the same year. Frank Sinatra, Deborah Kerr and Dean Martin starred in an implausible love triangle. *Marriage on the Rocks* for Nelson would be prophetic as his continuous philandering was having a detrimental effect on his marriage to Doreen Riddle, the mother of his seven children. They would be involved the messiest of divorces five years later.

The year 1965 was a busy one for Nelson with another drama called *A Rage to Live* directed by Walter Grauman (known for *633 Squadron*) which starred Suzanne Pleshette as a married woman with an addiction for having sex with casual partners. Film Score Monthly's review said, "Nelson Riddle weaved Ferrante and Teicher's title tune throughout his underscore, generating considerable sympathy for Grace, the lead character. A more up-tempo jazz style number was also included called 'Kiss Me Pumpkin'. This was Nelson's own composition, designed to add a sleazy feel to Grace's numerous sexual encounters."

Next, a collaboration with ace producer/director Howard Hawks for Paramount saw Nelson score *Red Line 7000* which is the story of three racing drivers and three women who constantly have to worry for the lives of their partners.

Quentin Tarantino is a fan of this film. "If I were to direct a racing movie, I would look to mimic a lot of that sixties AIP flavour. I would draw inspiration from Howard Hawk's *Red Line 7000*. It's not pretentious like *Grand Prix* and stuff, but the story is not dissimilar."

Nelson's composition for the opening theme illustrates what the picture is all about—danger and speed! It is as fast-moving as the cars depicted on the racetrack.

The following year saw the release of *Batman: The Movie,* starring Adam West as Batman and Burt Ward as Robin. This movie release was off the back of their successful TV series. A strong supporting cast saw Cesar Romero as The Joker, Burgess Meredith as The Penguin with Lee Meriwether as Cat-woman and Frank Gorshin as The Riddler. What better musician to score a film with The Riddler as a main character than Nelson Riddle? Kapow!

Nelson's prolific film work continued in 1967 with *The Spy In The Green Hat* which was a feature film version of the cult TV series *The Man From U.N.C.L.E* which supercharged the careers of Robert Vaughn (Napoleon Solo) and David McCallum (Ilya Kuryakin). They were joined in the cast by tough-guy Jack Palance (*Shane*) and Janet Leigh (*Psycho)*. Nelson's score, not considered to be one of his best, was not well received by the producer who publicly pronounced he was extremely disappointed with Nelson's work.

That same year saw Nelson re-united with Howard Hawks for a large budget western, *El Dorado*, which had the "big two", John Wayne and Robert Mitchum, take top billing, as well as introducing James Caan who played a young, top-hatted gambler. The film theme composed by Nelson is typical western fayre, there is no mistaking that. It is sung by George Alexander and the Mellomen.

The lyrics were adapted from an Edgar Allan Poe poem:

In sunshine and shadow, from darkness till noon
Over mountains that reach from the sky to the moon
A man with a dream that will never let go
Keeps searching to find El Dorado

There was also an instrumental version released which adds a new dynamic to the tune. The film itself sees hired gun John Wayne join forces with an old friend, Sheriff J.P. Harrah, played by Robert Mitchum. The story is similar to *Rio Bravo,* also directed by Hawks, with the Mitchum role played by Dean Martin.

Nelson was also involved with a number of less notable pictures like the 1969 releases *The Maltese Bippy* and *The Great Bank Robbery*. Then came the Alan Jay Lerner musical *Paint Your Wagon.* This film was a twenty-million-dollar budget affair and had a main cast of Lee Marvin, Clint Eastwood, and Jean Seberg with a strong supporting cast, including actor/tenor Harve Presnell. Nelson had to coach Lee Marvin and Clint Eastwood who were not natural singers.

Christopher Riddle: "As a kid, I used to deliver liquor to Lee Marvin. He would always give a generous tip. Years later, when I was performing in Dad's band, I was privileged to attend the red-carpet film premiere in

London of the film *Paint Your Wagon*, a musical which was had been a huge hit on Broadway.

"My father composed the Oscar nominated score and was instrumental in getting Lee Marvin to sing 'Wandrin' Star', as only he could 'sing' it. Lee questioned my dad on how he was going to be able to do it. Dad just said, 'Don't worry, Lee, we'll figure something out.'

El Dorado The big two John Wayne and Robert Mitchum.
Photograph courtesy Paramount Pictures.

The song was top of the charts for many weeks."

The only Oscar nomination the film received was Nelson's for the Oscar for Best Music Score of a Musical Picture. Still, it wasn't to be, another nomination but no wins!

Paint Your Wagon starring Clint Eastwood, Lee Marvin and Jean Seberg. Photograph courtesy of Paramount Pictures.

Film Trivia:

"The film was not the huge box-office success that the producers had hoped it would be. Clint Eastwood's experiences on this movie inspired him to form his own production company, Malpaso, saying that working on this movie had shown him how not to make a movie!

"The shoot attracted local vagrants and hippies, who stole food and supplies from the set. Director Joshua Logan cast them as extras, though they refused his instructions to cut their hair or wear period clothing. Eventually, the extras organized a makeshift union, demanding twenty-five dollar a day payments and commissary bags full of food for fellow hippies. Logan, aggravated by an overlong shoot and lacking replacements, gave in to their demands." Source: IMDb.

Hy Averback's *The Great Bank Robbery* was a Warner Bros/Seven Arts production released the same year. This comedy western set in 1880 centres on plans to rob a top-security bank situated in the town of Friendly, Texas. One of the screenwriters was William Peter Blatty who is known for the cult horror film *The Exorcist*.

Nelson was an orchestrator for Barbra Streisand's film debut in *Funny Girl* in 1968, one of the few actresses to win an Oscar on her film debut. The film was a huge box office success but was riven by internal disputes. Streisand ruffled a lot of feathers. It was also filmed in the middle of the six-day war in the Middle East. Omar Sharif who played Nick Arnstein was Egyptian, so tensions were especially high when he and Streisand shared more intimate moments. Nelson was to score Streisand's next film, replacing Neal Hefti who was replaced at the request of Streisand who said, "I want Nelson Riddle."

The film in question was *On A Clear Day You Can See Forever,* where he served as the film's music supervisor, arranger and conductor. It was released in 1970. French actor Yves Montand starred opposite Streisand.

Producer Koch found Streisand challenging but agreed to her "request" to bring Nelson on board. Nelson and Streisand worked well together musically. He was fascinated by her vocal instrument which he referred to as an oboe. When writing arrangements, he regarded the vocalist as being another instrument in the orchestra.

According to the 1974 biography, *Barbra Streisand: The First Decade*, this was first envisaged as a three-hour "road show" extravaganza and included many sequences of Daisy's other lives (photos of which were printed in some pre-release promotions), but Director Vincente Minnelli and the studio felt it would be too long, especially since musicals had already begun to fail at the box-office. In addition to all but the briefest of Jack Nicholson's scenes being cut, a musical number sung by him, "Who Is There Among Us Who Knows?", with Barbra humming in harmony, was also cut, as well as a duet between Larry Blyden and Barbra Streisand.

Christopher Riddle: "The music department at Paramount was being run by Bill Stinson. He rated Dad very highly as a primo film score arranger and composer. I wish my dad had done an album with Barbra. They both would have done it, but schedules didn't permit. Another regret is I wish he had done an album with Tony Bennett. My father didn't have management as such; he wouldn't pay for it. A false economy. His career needed direction."

Rosemary (Riddle) Acerra: "One of the movies Dad worked on was *On a Clear Day You Can See Forever* starring Barbra Streisand, Yves Montand, and Jack Nicholson. I was back from college at the time and was able to visit the post-production suite and see first-hand how they synced the music to the film. It was a fascinating experience."

Film trivia:

"Paramount offered Yves Montand two hundred thousand dollars for the role of Dr. Marc Chabot. Uneasy about playing another Latin lover, Montand made a counteroffer of four hundred thousand dollars, 'just to see what they say'. To his surprise, Paramount accepted.

"Richard Harris was first choice as the doctor, but after many arguments with Barbra Streisand, he left the movie.

"It is one of the very rare Hollywood musicals where the two main characters do not kiss each other." Source: IMDb

The film's soundtrack is well worth a listen if only for Streisand's closing chorus of the title song, holding the note of "Forever and Ever More" for a period in excess of twenty seconds!

In 1974, *The Great Gatsby* was released by Paramount. Robert Evans was the producer. Truman Capote was chosen to write the screenplay, but his first draft was rejected, and he was fired then replaced by Francis Ford Coppola.

Christopher Riddle: "My father switched a lot of his attention to writing for films in the 60's and 70's. I remember going with him to Paramount studios and attending a lunch with producer David Merrick when they were filming *The Great Gatsby* starring Robert Redford and Mia Farrow. That was in 1974. He recorded the score at Glen Glenn Studios. The music was added as is the norm at the post-production stage, but Dad was always kept in the loop by the producer and the director Jack Clayton from the early stages of the film's development. My father finally got recognised, winning the Oscar for Best Motion Picture Score having been nominated several times previously."

The song "What'll I Do?" which is heard in the film, was written by Irving Berlin. Nelson Riddle did the adaptation for the film and years later was engaged by pop star Linda Ronstadt to arrange her version of the popular standard.

The Great Gatsby The Oscar at last for Nelson!
Photograph courtesy of Paramount Pictures.

Mia Farrow wrote that the main reason she couldn't create on-screen chemistry with Robert Redford was because of Redford's total absorption in the Watergate scandals that were rocking Washington, D.C. at the time. Farrow said Redford spent all of his free time locked in his trailer watching the political scandal unfold on television. Two years later, Redford played Watergate reporter Bob Woodward in *All the President's Men*. Source: IMDb

Diahann Carroll presents the Oscar to Nelson for Best Motion Picture score for *The Great Gatsby*. Photograph courtesy of The Nelson Riddle Memorial Library Arizona State University.

The film wasn't received well by the critics, although it was profitable at the box office grossing $21 million dollars to date. It won two Academy Awards (Oscars) one for Theoni V. Aldredge for best costume design but important for Nelson as he won the Oscar for Best Music, Scoring Original Song Score and/or Adaption, to be precise.

After so many nominations, he finally achieved recognition from the academy. The Oscar was presented to Nelson at the 1975 Academy Awards ceremony by singer/actress Diahann Carroll of *Carmen Jones* fame, latterly of TV's *Dynasty*.

Sadly, Nelson's children are unable to covet the award in their own homes as Nelson's second wife, Naomi, saw fit to snub the family and donate that and many other items to Arizona State University as part of the Nelson Riddle Memorial Library collection, which she set up. Quite why she decided to set up the library without the involvement of Nelson's children is unclear.

Throughout the seventies, Nelson continued to conduct his orchestra and play as many live dates as possible, although the concert tour dates were not so readily available to him as those for the likes of Henry Mancini who was the first call for the "hot" vocalists of the time like Johnny Mathis, but it was his TV and film work that kept the Nelson Riddle name out there. Those of us of a certain age will remember the many rolling TV and film credits of the sixties and seventies showing "Music by Nelson Riddle". The name itself conjured up an image of cool, dynamic music associated with the productions of the period. Hollywood was kind to Nelson during this era of the swinging sixties and sexy seventies. It was regular work that enabled Nelson to "stuff dollar bills into holes", his regular reply to people who asked after how things were going at the time.

Christopher Riddle: "We were doing the AFI (American Film Institute) Awards. My father was music director for that for the first ten years. George Stevens Jr. produced it. We were doing that show, and I think it was William Wyler that year who got the lifetime achievement award. He directed Olivia De Haviland in

The Heiress where she won an Oscar. She did a favourite movie of mine with Alan Ladd and David Ladd called *The Proud Rebel.* Jerome Moross wrote the music; he did *The Big Country,* of course. I told Joan Fontaine about my meeting with her sister—this was about 17 years later. She just shrugged her shoulders."

"I used to deliver liquor to Laurence Harvey who played opposite Frank in *The Manchurian Candidate.* He was building a beach house off the Malibu highway on Carbon beach—we lived in Carbon Canyon. He was sitting on the second floor. It was just framework at the time, and I would deliver him champagne in an ice bucket. He was sitting there entertaining the carpenters as they were putting the house together around him. Another actor, Louis Hayward, had a house just round the bend from there. I used to deliver to him too. His son Dana went to school with me at Our Lady of Malibu. On the other side of the curve was where Lloyd Bridges (*High Noon*, TV's *Sea Hunt*, *Airport*) lived. He used a Royal Master regulator. He played Mike Nelson! In filming *Sea Hunt* fight scenes, they always cut the left hose, which is the exhaust, not the right one where the air comes in. I was mixing with these people in the main because of my father's status in Hollywood at the time.

Frank banned *Manchurian Candidate* after Kennedy got killed, and *Suddenly* wasn't seen until recently because Frank played a character who was going to assassinate the President."

The year 1976 saw a number of TV series added to the list, notably *Executive Suite, City of Angels.* The big screen saw a couple of tribute movies, *That's Entertainment, Part II.* Many of Nelson's scores were highlighted in the film in a number of film clips shown.

Several other films and TV series followed to close the seventies. Other film scores and orchestrations included a *Kiss Before Dying (1956),* a film-noir crime thriller starring Robert Wagner, Jeffrey Hunter and Joanne Woodward. *Hell's Bloody Devils* is a movie released in 1970 and one of a group of largely forgettable movies Nelson was involved with in the seventies. *Hell's Bloody Devils* was shot in 1967 but released three years later, probably due to lack of funding for the post-production aspect. Nelson composed the theme music. The film is notable for exceptionally low rating reviews on IMDb. Rivalling that rating was *Going Coconuts,* a comedy adventure vehicle for Donny and Marie Osmond, sadly one that crashed at the box office. The soundtrack includes "Polynesian Medley" and "On the Shelf" sung by Donnie and Marie. It edges out *Devils* with an IMDb rating of 4.2/10.

In 1976, Nelson was the conductor and music arranger for the title music for the American Film Institute's documentary *America at the Movies* directed by George Stevens Jr. This was a compilation of scenes from 83 films, divided into 5 segments: The Land, The Cities, The Families, The Wars, and The Spirit.

In '78, Nelson scored *Harper Valley PTA.* This was a movie inspired by Jeannie C. Riley's hit record. Although not critically acclaimed, box office returns were good. The original vinyl soundtrack included a re-release of Riley's hit single which was used to promote the movie. As an un-credited extra, this marked the film debut of Woody Harrelson. There was a spin-off TV series in 1981 where Barbara Eden reprised her role of Stella Johnson.

A story of a cult but not a cult film, *Guyana: Cult of the Damned,* released in 1979 is about Reverend Jim Jones, a church minister who orders his followers to commit suicide. The name of the central character was changed to James Johnson as this was an unauthorised version. Nelson was one of several composers hired to provide the music. A strong cast includes Stuart Whitman, Yvonne De Carlo, Gene Barry and Bradford Dillman. Loosely based on a true story, that's about all there is to say.

Rascal Dazzle (1980) was a series of memorable clips from *Our Gang comedies* aka *The Little Rascals*, the cast featured Jackie Cooper and the story was narrated by Jerry Lewis. Of course, Nelson provided the music.

Nelson teamed up with David Merrick (prod. *The Great Gatsby*) later that year working with director Don Siegel to write the score for a movie called *Rough Cut* starring Burt Reynolds, Lesley Anne-Down and David Niven. It was a rom-com caper about sophisticated jewel thieves, and Nelson's score epitomised that.

Burt Reynolds was at the peak of his fame at the time this movie was made, and David Niven's new career as a best-selling author (*The Moon's a Balloon*) meant his stock was back on the rise too. However, neither was able to rescue this movie. Nelson's score which were mainly arrangements of Duke Ellington tunes had a poor review from Roger Ebert saying they ranged from very suave to crushingly obvious, citing the well-known classic "Caravan" as a case in point. This was in stark contrast with other reviews which gave Nelson's score a five-star rating. With his health now failing him, *Rough Cut* was to be Nelson's penultimate film score.

His last film hurrah was the comedy *Chattanooga Choo Choo* released in 1984, a year before Nelson passed. It starred George Kennedy, a football club owner who stood to make an inheritance of one million dollars

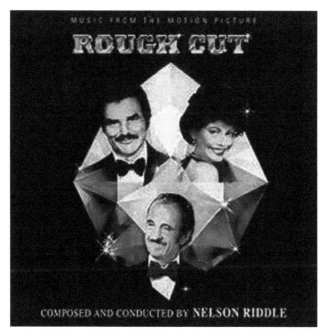

The soundtrack album to the movie *Rough Cut.*
Photograph courtesy of Paramount Pictures.

provided he could restore an old train, the *Chattanooga Choo Choo,* and make the twenty-four hour journey from Chattanooga to New York. The film came and went largely un-noticed although Nelson's score was well received.

It was a long and, in most instances, a distinguished film career, whether it was writing scores for large budget feature films or composing for lesser funded movies.

7. TELEVISION MAN

When the world crashes into my living room
Television made me what I am

Nelson had a top ten hit with *Route 66,* the theme from the popular TV series. It was the first TV theme to hit the charts.

Television work at this time for Nelson was in abundance. In addition to *Route 66,* he was composing for the award-winning *Profiles in Courage,* an NBC TV dramatization of John F. Kennedy's book. Nelson used the tune "The Boys from Wexford", this being a tune about JFK's ancestral town in Ireland. JFK liked it so much, he requested it be used for the theme for that show. Sadly, Kennedy had been assassinated a year before the show aired, by which time Nelson's theme tune was re-named the "John F. Kennedy March".

Christopher Riddle: "On school holidays, I went to Catholic school and we sometimes had holidays mid-week to celebrate one saint or another. My father had an office at Screen Gems at Beechwood. I would go with him and watch a *Route 66* episode. One of the engineers used to offer out chocolates to guests. They weren't very edible as they were made of rubber! They were used in the programme. I remember there was a little Italian restaurant not far away from there called Naples; it was on Gower Street. I used to go there on my own for lunch, and the maître d' knew me, so lunch was on Screen Gems (or Screen germs as it was affectionately known). It was great. I used to have this delicious spaghetti and meatballs every time. I guess I would have been around twelve years of age."

Bill Haley is generally regarded as bringing rock and roll into the public domain with his chart-topping number "Rock Around The Clock". A young rocker called Elvis "the pelvis" Presley then took charge and quickly established himself as the king of rock. Although the advent of rock and roll did nothing to enhance Nelson's career, it did not destroy it. In fact, he was forced to switch his focus. This enabled Nelson more freedom to express himself, and the results are a number of excellent compositions.

This seismic shift in musical tastes was bad news for Nelson Riddle. Whilst the numerous collaborations he had made, most notably with Sinatra but also Nat Cole, Ella Fitzgerald, Rosemary Clooney, and others, were to become an integral part of American popular music, this new genre attracted a new following.

Nelson continued to be musical director on a number of TV shows, but his work as an arranger for vocalist recorded work started to decline. Nelson had a blue-collar work ethic, however, and he hardly ever turned down any work, be it live concerts, smaller gigs, one-off arrangements, and TV/film scores.

"Composed and conducted by Nelson Riddle" became a familiar sight on the credits on many TV screens during this period. Once again, the prolific arranger didn't disappoint, and his focus would be pertinent to the particular characteristics and theme of a number of the shows in question.

In 1959, Fidel Castro came to power in Cuba. US President Eisenhower signed the Hawaii Admission Act into law, and Hawaii became the 50th state of the USA. It was also notable for iconic movie releases such as *Some Like It Hot, Ben Hur,* and the Hitchcock masterpiece *North by Northwest* starring Cary Grant and Eva Marie Saint.

That year also saw the introduction of a new hard hitting crime series from CBS called *The Untouchables,* which had TV and film actor Robert Stack in the lead role as Eliot Ness. The series was produced by Desilu, headed by Desi Arnaz and Lucille Ball.

The show concentrated on the true-life story of Ness and his squad of treasury agents that helped bring down the notorious bootlegger Al Capone. *The Untouchables* ran for four straight years ending in 1963. Robert Stack won an Emmy Award for Best Actor in a Dramatic Series in 1960. The show attracted a number of notable guest appearances: actors such as Charles Bronson, Joan Blondell, James Coburn, Robert Duvall, Cloris Leachman, Lee Marvin, Claire Trevor, Barbara Stanwyck and Robert Redford, to name but a few.

Whilst it became an award-winning drama, it drew some harsh criticism from no less than Frank Sinatra and other members of the Italian American community, who felt it stereo-typed them as mobsters and gangsters.

The Capone family unsuccessfully sued CBS and Desilu for the way the Capone family was depicted. In fact, producer Desi Arnaz (who attended the same high school as Al Capone's son Albert) had to deal with an ongoing public outcry from associated trade unions. Arnaz met their criticisms head on with a three-point plan to modify some of the storylines pertaining to the image of Italian American characters.

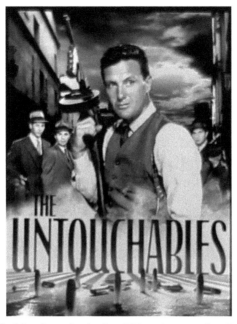

The Untouchables Award winning TV series starring Robert Stack.
Photograph Desilu productions.

Nelson recording session with Rosemary Clooney. Photograph
The Nelson Riddle Memorial Library Arizona State University.

The series was hallmarked by the clipped narration by gossip columnist Walter Winchell together with its *film noir* theme and haunting music score composed by our man Riddle.

Robert Stack started out his film career in the 1930's as a song and dance man. His comments on Nelson's music echoes his knowledge and experience: "Nelson Riddle's score does a great deal to create the undercurrent of excitement that characterizes our show. It is music with a heartbeat that captures perfectly the suspense and impending violence of the action."

I don't know about you, but I always see a movie or TV series as being a marriage between the story and the music. Many of the most memorable films and TV shows have a great score which resonates with the viewer. Nelson's main theme for *The Untouchables* is in that category. When you listen to it, you can understand what Stack is alluding to. The tune is slightly off-beat and has a spooky vocal backing. Three other tracks on the soundtrack album have a vintage jazz feel of the speakeasy combos of the period of prohibition from 1919 to 1933. The album released by Capitol consists of several tunes with a "Ness" added, such as "Tender-ness", "Reckless-ness", "Wistful-ness". All of which exude that music heartbeat that Robert Stack refers to.

There was a spin-off TV (full length) movie that Nelson scored titled *The Gun of Zangara*. Stack starred again as the intrepid treasury agent, Eliot Ness. This was a dramatization of true events leading to the attempted assassination of President-elect FD Roosevelt at Miami Beach in 1933. The movie is highly rated on IMDb with a viewer rating of 8.6/10. There is little evidence of Nelson's score, but I am sure he produced a tune in keeping with the atmospheric suspense theme he composed for *The Untouchables.*

At this time for Nelson, commissions for TV and film scores were coming thick and fast. The following year, 1960, was the year Real Madrid thrashed Eintracht Frankfurt 7-3 in the European Cup Final at Glasgow's Hampden Park. John F Kennedy won the Democratic presidential nomination for the US general election, which he would contest against the then current vice-president Richard Nixon.

The year 1960 also brought to us a classic TV series called *Route 66,* a road-trip drama starring Martin Milner as Tod and George Maharis as Buz. They portray two buddies who decide to take the legendary Route 66 highway in a Chevrolet Corvette convertible (there were only two Corvettes available to them so the accent was on safe driving), taking work where they can get it and getting into various escapades?? as a result.

Martin Milner beat several actors, including Robert Redford, for the role of Tod, although Redford was to appear as a guest star in a future episode. Once again, this was a TV series rich with well-known guest stars such as David Janssen, Jessica Walter, Martin Sheen, Stefanie Powers, Jack Lord, Sessue Hayakawa, Joan Crawford, Lew Ayres, amongst others.

Nelson was hired by producer Herbert Leonard to do the incidental music for each episode (the series ran from 1960 to 1963). The main theme was to be the classic song "Route 66" composed and performed by Bobby Troup. However, Leonard's negotiations with Troup over fees and royalties were long and tortuous, leading Leonard to pull out altogether. The show was due to start within the next week, so Leonard approached Nelson.

Christopher Riddle: "Bert Leonard explained the Bobby Troup situation and asked Dad to come up with a theme in the next few days. As always, Dad worked best under extreme pressure. The result was his theme tune for *Route 66* which was I believe was the first TV theme to make the top thirty on the Billboard charts."

Naked City was a highly rated TV police drama that ran from 1958-59, was cancelled, then resurrected in 1960 and enjoyed a successful run for the next three years. Nelson was brought in to compose incidental music and composed a new theme tune used for the final season. George Duning and Billy May wrote the other themes for 1958/59 and 1960/62, the latter being the most recognisable tune of the three.

Nelson's eldest son, Nelson "Skip" Riddle III, spent a lot of time on set for the last season and met the star of the show, Paul Burke, who played Detective Adam Flint. Skip remembers his father and the actor hit it off as they both shared an interest in maths games.

Skip takes up the story: "I got to know Paul quite well. He and Dad used to spend their break time doing math puzzles. Dad had an engineer's mind and enjoyed complex puzzles. He had complex thoughts which correlated with the rich tapestry of sounds he created, perfect for arranging music, although my father did have some trouble writing melodies. I guess to use Walt Disney's phrase, Dad could be described as an imagineer.

"Musically, he and I were on a different page at the time. I idolised Elvis, Jerry Lee Lewis and Chuck Berry. Dad hated that—he had a great run, but rock and roll finished that. He had to re-invent himself. I recall Frank (Sinatra) saying at the time, 'How come they come to my shows but don't buy my records?' I had studied piano myself and had a natural ear; in fact, I had my own group, The Malibu Men. 'Cookie' Cole (Natalie), Dennis of Carmen's Dragon and on drums was Daryll Dragon of Captain and Tennille. However, I got distracted and music wasn't the life or career for me."

Sam Benedict is an American legal drama that aired on NBC from September 1962 to March 1963. The series was created and executively produced by E. Jack Neumann.

The stories are based on real-life lawyer Jacob "Jake" Ehrlich, who served as technical consultant for the series.[1] It starred Edmond O'Brien as flamboyant San Francisco attorney Sam Benedict. Richard Rust portrayed his 24-year-old associate, Henry "Hank" Tabor. Joan Tompkins co-starred in all episodes as Trudy Wagner. Most episodes followed two story lines: first Benedict's case and then Tabor's. It had many notable guest stars such as Vera Miles and Claude Rains. Who can forget him as the French Vichy police chief in the classic war romance *Casablanca,* which starred Humphrey Bogart and Ingrid Bergman.

Nelson composed the catchy theme tune for *Sam Benedict* which was later released on CD.

Christopher Riddle: "A neighbour of ours was actress Vera Miles who did some wonderful films like *The Wrong Man, The Man Who Shot Liberty Valance* (with Lee Marvin). I went to primary school with her daughter Debra. I went to their house quite a lot to hang out and play. Many other film stars of the era lived close by, people like Burgess Meredith, that brilliant character actor who played the Penguin in the TV series *Batman* and the movie version where my dad wrote the score, and much later in his career, he played the manager of Sylvester Stallone's *Rocky.*"

Profiles in Courage is an American historical anthology series that was telecast weekly on NBC from November 8, 1964 to May 9, 1965 (Sundays, 6:30-7:30pm, Eastern). The series was based on the Pulitzer Prize winning 1956 book, *Profiles in Courage* by then senator John F. Kennedy (and Ted Sorensen). Kennedy, as US president, had been assassinated the previous November.

The series lasted for 26 episodes, each of which would feature a figure from American history who took an unpopular stand during a critical moment in the nation's history. Seven of the eight senators from Kennedy's book were profiled, with the exception being Mississippi's Lucius Quintus Cincinnatus Lamarr.

The tune was re-named "The John F. Kennedy March" in honour of the deceased president and was recorded by Nelson subsequently for CD release. When Kennedy visited his ancestral home in Wexford, he was so impressed by this tune that he instructed that it be used as the opening theme to the TV series. Nelson duly carried out those wishes to the letter but sadly by that time Kennedy was dead.

Nelson scored some of the episodes for *Tarzan,* an NBC series starring Ron Ely which ran from 1966-68. For the shooting of the first season, Ron Ely performed his own stunts and sustained several different injuries including singeing (that's singeing not singing) his arms and legs running through a burning village, being bitten on the forehead by a "tame" lion, falling off a vine, and falling twenty-five feet and dislocating his shoulder. Nelson's score was less dramatic but still effective.

Nelson kept busy composing instrumental covers of a number of TV themes such as *Martin Kane,* a bizarre detective series that transferred from radio to television. The show's sponsor was a tobacco company, so they sought to include visits to tobacco shops as part of the storyline. It ran from 1949-54. Another such cover released by Capitol was *Markham,* another TV 'tec, this was a more lavish affair. It starred Ray Milland who played a lawyer turned detective who, although based in New York City, solved crimes anywhere in the world. Nelson's composition is equally lavish with a full orchestra. A strong piano presence is supported by strings and backing vocals. A nice theme tune.

Nelson was musical director for the *Smothers Brothers Comedy Hour* between 1967 and 1969. The show was cancelled by CBS after Tom Smothers lobbied members of Congress about corporate censorship. CBS president, Robert Wood, rattled by the bad publicity acted quickly, and fired them.

However, Christopher Riddle has a different take on things: "I remember George Sunga. He was producer of the *Smothers Brothers Comedy Hour.* They had gotten themselves cancelled because of their anti-Vietnam war position. We all had lunch at Musso and Franks. My dad was furious because he had turned down the Carol Burnett Show because he was too busy. Burnett's show continued for another seven or eight years. That show was made for him, far better suited than the Smothers Brothers. I remember years later we played a job for the Smothers Brothers at the Aladdin in Vegas; it had a big ballroom at the back. We played there for just a week."

Emergency! was created and produced by Jack Webb and Robert A. Cinader, who had also created the police dramas *Adam-12* and *Dragnet.* In the show's original TV-movie pilot, the series aimed to be a realistic portrayal of emergency medical services (EMS). Pioneering EMS leader James O. Page served as a technical advisor and the two main actors underwent some paramedic training.

Jack Webb's (Sgt Joe Friday in *Dragnet*) personal life was better defined by his love of jazz than his interest in police work. He had a collection of more than 6,000 jazz recordings. Webb's own recordings reached cult status, especially his deadpan delivery of "Try A Little Tenderness". His lifelong interest in the cornet allowed him to move easily in the jazz culture, where he met his wife, singer and actress Julie London. Webb came to know Nelson quite well from moving in those circles and engaged his services as the composer of the theme music and to score the series, although Billy May did contribute some of the incidental music. The theme tune is a brash, brassy affair, all guns blazing a fast tempo to mirror the speed associated with emergency services. Emergency ran from 1972 through to 1977. Nelson was employed again by Webb for the sci-fi series *Project UFO* loosely based on *Project Blue Book*. The series ran for two seasons from 1978/9, totalling 26 episodes. Nelson's credit was prominently displayed as befits his stature, and his theme music is out of this world!

Joseph Waumbaugh's *The Blue Knight* was aired in 1973 as a TV movie. It starred William Holden as Bumper Morgan, a veteran Los Angeles street cop. He is due to retire after twenty years but still battles crime as if it were his first day on the beat. Holden's co-star was Lee Remick. This was Holden's debut acting in a TV mini-series.

Nelson composed the opening theme and incidental music. This was a classy production all round, winning four Emmy awards and a Golden Globe for Lee Remick as Best TV actress.

Mini-series were the new TV phenomenon in the 1970's and *Seventh Avenue* was a Universal release in 1977; there were three episodes in total. There were a number of guest stars including Ray Milland and Gloria Grahame with Anne Archer and Jane Seymour in the main cast. Nelson was engaged to write the score.

Nelson was appointed as musical director for *The Carpenters: Music, Music, Music* (1980). It was a television special charting a salute to American popular music and composers. It was a fitting way to start a new decade. This fifth and final ABC Carpenter's special had Karen and Richard Carpenter flanked by Ella Fitzgerald, John Davidson and Nelson Riddle with his orchestra. Nelson arranged and conducted a medley, "1980 Carpenters Medley". The show received a 9.6/10 review rating on IMDb.

8. WHEN YOUR LOVER HAS GONE

What good is the scheming, the planning and dreaming
That comes with each new love affair

We are all human beings, some more human than others, of course, but that's another story, for another time. Seriously, as a human species, we are fallible, and we are all different, thank goodness. Here I write about some difficult times in the Nelson Riddle story. I hope I have done so in a sensitive and non-judgmental fashion.

Nelson once said, "Music to me is sex. It's all tied up somehow, and the rhythm of sex is the heartbeat." He explained, "I always have some woman in mind for each song I arrange; it could be a reminiscence of some past romantic experience or just a dream-scene I build in my own imagination. The tempo of the heartbeat, that's the tempo that strikes people easiest because without their knowing it, they are moving to that pace all their waking hours."

Nelson's workload in the Capitol years was humongous. We have established that working at break-neck speed under pressure was part of Nelson's DNA, and he came up with the goods time after time. Also, we mustn't forget that he was a recording artist in his own right, scoring Billboard charts with four instrumental hits. He was therefore having to balance the composition of his instrumental orchestrations with writing arrangements for Capitol's large roster of singing stars. This excessive workload was a personal choice, yet because of his blue-collar work ethic, he was able to fulfil both functions.

Doreen Riddle during one of their many arguments once said to Nelson, "All you ever think of is music and sex," to which Nelson replied, "That's true. After all, what else is there?"

In the early days of their marriage, Doreen did everything for Nelson whilst he was trying to establish a career in the music industry. In fact, Tommy Dorsey would have welcomed Nelson back in a heartbeat after his stint with Uncle Sam, but Doreen pointed out to her husband that it may not be a smart career move, especially if Nelson wanted to be recognised as an arranger and composer in his own right. Nelson's work ethic together with his memories of the dark days of the Great Depression where jobs were non-existent and money scarce, meant he was willing to seriously consider Dorsey's offer. Fortunately, he took Doreen's advice and sought other avenues to advance his career. Doreen and Nelson had seven children together, Nelson III "Skip", Rosemary, Christopher, Bettina, Cecily, Maureen and Leonora Celeste who sadly died, aged six months.

The death triggered a deep depression in Doreen Riddle, who struggled with both depression and alcoholism.

Although the Riddles went on to have two more children, Cecily in 1960 and Maureen in 1962, Doreen's drinking and Nelson's serial philandering were a toxic cocktail which led to a corrosive effect on their marriage. They began to argue constantly, and on one specific occasion, the children overheard them from the bedrooms upstairs.

Christopher Riddle: "I heard Dad say, 'You had to have all those children.' At which point I said to my siblings, 'He means you, not me.' I remember thinking about his comment at a later time. 'You had to have all those children?' Surely, my father had something to do with it?"

Nelson had several dalliances with women who were in his workspace and who seemed attracted by his slight aloofness and sorrowful look. "He's with that blonde again" was a constant reply from Doreen when the children asked about the whereabouts of their father. The blonde in question at that time would invariably be singer Rosemary Clooney.

Their affair which was to last a number of years, was anything but discreet.

Christopher Riddle recalls: "I remember my mother overindulging in alcohol. It was not a happy period for her. She was devoted to my father and did everything for him. He commented that sometimes he felt he was the eighth child. When he started the fooling around, that led to her drinking to excess. She used to say, 'Your father is with that blonde again.' There were many big rows downstairs. I think Rosemary Clooney was very close to becoming my stepmother!"

Clooney, seven years younger than Nelson, was born on 29th June in 1928, which was a leap year and was notable for Scotsman John Logie Baird demonstrating the first colour TV transmission from Glasgow. It was also the year Eliot Ness headed up the prohibition unit in Chicago. Clooney came to the public's attention with her hit record "Come On-A My House" which was produced by the prolific Mitch Miller at Columbia. She went on to enjoy further recording success and starring in a number of movies such as *White Christmas* with Bing Crosby. She was married to actor Jose Ferrer at the time of her affair with Nelson. Their marriage was a very fraught union with Ferrer cheating on Clooney on numerous occasions.

Clooney with her slightly husky, bubbly voice had a unique appeal. It was not surprising that when Nelson got the call to be musical director on the first Rosemary Clooney show that Clooney and Nelson became friends. It was nothing more than that to begin with. As time progressed, they realised their respective birthdays were little over a week apart, so they started to celebrate them, initially with a group of friends, then as a couple. Their romance blossomed. Clooney could rely on Naomi Tenenholtz, Nelson's secretary at the time, to book a suite at the Plaza Hotel for their joint birthday celebrations and clandestine meetings. It didn't take long however for either party to show their love for each other. It was a very public airing. This was evident every week in the TV footage of the show. Clooney had Nelson join her in many musical sketches where they would openly flirt with one another. He was almost becoming her co-star on the show.

She describes him in her autobiography, *Girl Singer,* as "the best singer who ever lived, because you know what to do on any given word and/or particular note. What you write conveys exactly what I'm feeling. Exactly!" She went to say that "Nelson didn't embellish a lyric or even enhance it. He ennobled it". Clooney was clearly smitten with Nelson and this feeling was very much reciprocated. She was attracted by his dry, sardonic wit yet intense sadness. Clooney loved to make Nelson laugh, drawing out that warm instinctive smile of his.

Christopher Riddle remembers that his dad didn't use a wallet, opting to stuff twenty-dollar bills in his pockets, usually all scrunched up. A number of these dollar bills fell out of his pockets, never to be recovered. "Rosemary Clooney decided to gift my father a gold money clip with the inscription, 'If you lose another twenty dollars, this time you'll hear it!'"

Nelson returned his love to Clooney through his orchestrations which put her limited vocal abilities into the top echelon of female singers. The Rosemary Clooney show ran from 1955 through to 1957. There were forty-two episodes in total. Nelson was musical director for exactly half of those. The fast-working, over-burdened Nelson was taking every bit of work he was offered.

Nelson and Doreen's marriage disintegrated just as the arranger's career hit its peak.

Rosemary Acerra: "They let Dad's success destroy them. When they were struggling, they were happy."

Clooney and Nelson combined to conjure up an upbeat collection, *Rosie Solves the Swingin' Riddle*. By 1960, they had fallen in love, and in the following year, he chose to commemorate their not-so-secret romance by writing her a sumptuous album of lavish arrangements called *Love*.

Rosemary Clooney in her book admits that her relationship with Nelson was a long-standing extra-marital affair. Naomi, as Nelson's secretary, helped to carry out that deceit still further by renting an apartment after their music engagements were finished for the evening; this enabled them to have numerous overnight stopovers.

Clooney and Nelson had twelve children between them by their respective partners, yet they constantly talked about separating from their spouses and setting up home together. The couple were like a couple of love-struck teenagers. They sought advice from Frank Sinatra who told them both in no uncertain terms that the move was ill-advised and too complicated because of the number of children involved. Clooney was still keen, but it was Nelson who eventually recoiled at the prospect.

On one occasion after celebrating their respective birthdays, Clooney sensed there was something not quite right. "We can't carry on like this," Nelson stated out of the blue. Clooney hoped that Nelson meant that they would realise their plans to divorce their respective spouses and set up home together. They had discussed this many times, surely that's what he had meant? Nelson's silence when she followed up led Clooney to fear the worst. Nelson just repeated the same words. That was the end of the affair, one that both parties remembered and spoke about. Clooney was quite open about it in her autobiography, and Nelson admitted to friends in his darker moments that although he often thought about "Rosie", and he was only a few blocks away, he couldn't meet up with her; that the moment had passed. Nelson had tried to mend his marriage, but the damage was irretrievable. Doreen's drinking became more excessive with her mental wellbeing damaged to the point that she was hospitalised. Nelson's philandering continued, and numerous affairs or one-night stands ensued. There were rumours one of his affairs involved Margaret Whiting, the hit singer of the 1940/50's, with whom Nelson collaborated with on two albums. She had been one of the first signings for Capitol Records when it was founded in 1942.

Eleven years after Nelson's death, Clooney released *Dedicated to Nelson*, an album on the Concord Jazz label based on her work with Riddle on her TV show in 1956 and 1957.

"When we recorded *Love,* we were at the height of our feelings for one another. Tears ran down my face as I stood at the microphone. Every time he caught my eye over the heads of the orchestra, my heart leapt. Each song arrangement was more pointed and poignant than the last, *How Will I Remember You?* being one, and all of them laden with yearning, with regret lurking just around the corner."

Clooney had said that, except for the births of her children, her time with Nelson was the happiest period of her life.

As for Nelson, he said shortly before his death, "I still haven't lost the feeling for her. I've lived two or three miles from her for decades, and I never make the trip, and I'm not about to. I remember; that's all that's important. We cannot help each other at this point."

As a child, Rosemary Acerra was naturally upset about the affair. "I was very loyal to my mother," she said. "My mother believed so intently in my dad's talent, yet he was very shy about his talent." But as an adult, Acerra said she saw how complicated the situation was. "My mother and father had a very stormy marriage," Acerra said, "and at one point during the break-up of their marriage, Rosemary Clooney and Dad were too close. But it grew beyond the passionate feeling, and they were able to keep the friendship."

Christopher Riddle: "Mom died of cancer. Her marriage to Dad ended poorly. Aside from the excessive drinking, she must have smoked five packs of cigarettes a day. It was like suicide but over a long period; you don't put a gun to your head, but the end result is the same.

"I remember my father left home for good on April 20th 1968. My brother Skip got married that day.

We were returning from the ceremony to our house in the Malibu Colony. I was in the car with my father, and my mother had the rest of people in her Mercedes. As soon as we arrived, Dad said 'I'm leaving.' So, I helped Dad pack a few things.

Not long prior to that, my mother was bringing home random people from bars in Malibu. It was really bad. She brought home some people one night. My father was sleeping upstairs in the master bedroom, and my sisters were in bed. When I got home, I remember thinking, 'I don't want my family to come down in the morning and see these people sleeping on the couches,' as if it was my responsibility. I remembered one guy was a baseball player. He had a Buick Riviera. I got him up, got him coffee, walked him around and got him awake. I asked him to get in his car and told him to follow me, and I would get him on the highway. He was driving at a high rate of speed, and I was frightened he was going to ram me, so I had to leave him on the coast highway; otherwise, I was scared he was going to rear end me. I found out subsequently that this guy piled into this walk-over near Sunset Boulevard and killed himself."

In 1969, the inevitably messy divorce happened. Nelson duly married his long serving colleague and secretary Naomi Tenenholtz. Naomi did not get along with the Riddle children.

Rosemary Acerra: "She tried to separate us, but she was unsuccessful."

Naomi put her markers down early. Doreen was heard to say that "your father finally got his wish. He married his mother!" The children became isolated.

For most of the 1970's, Nelson's work comprised of writing for film and TV, together with any live dates. He was hired as musical director for the Julie Andrews Hour, a show consisting of Andrews singing and duetting with various guest stars. Star and musical director formed a close working relationship, although Andrews found Nelson to be a sad and forlorn figure, nicknaming him Eeyore after the character in A.A Milne's "Winnie The Pooh". Eeyore is characterized as pessimistic, gloomy, depressed and forlorn.

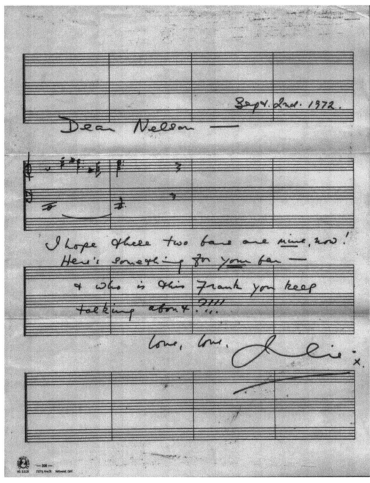

Julie Andrews note to Nelson during the period of her TV show *The Julie Andrews Hour*. Photograph courtesy of the Nelson Riddle Memorial Library Arizona State University.

Christopher Riddle: "Dad and Naomi finally bought a place on 1616 Bel Air Road. It was quite modest, and just before my father died, she started re-modelling the place, and she spent around seven hundred and fifty thousand dollars on it. She knew he was dying. To establish any sort of relationship with her, we would have to become sycophants. It was incumbent on that."

Naomi Riddle died in 1998, and it took the Riddle children, led by daughter Rosemary Acerra, until 2005 to regain control over their father's estate.

Christopher Riddle: "After Dad had passed, Naomi tried to stop me from working. When I was playing a job anywhere and the band had a break, I used to stay on the music stand to make sure nobody came and stole the music. Then she would threaten me with lawyers for using The Nelson Riddle Orchestra trademark. She thought she owned the name."

Nelson had a stint working on *Newhart* from 1982 up until he passed in 1985, 71 episodes in total. He was credited under the heading of composer of additional music. It was Henry Mancini who wrote the theme for the show.

Terry Woodson also worked in a similar capacity on this show. Terry recalls visiting Nelson:

"Around that time, we were doing the Bob Newhart TV show. He'd asked me to bring some score paper to the hospital so he could sketch out some stuff, but it never happened. He was too weak. He didn't look frail, but his voice and gestures were weak.

"I had a number of dealings with his wife Naomi. Sometimes I was invited into the home. I had known her as Nelson's secretary. The cat jumped up on my lap, which he never did with anyone else, so she liked me after that. After Nelson died, she said she was coming after the music. She boxed some stuff.

"There was a guy called Mike Berkowitz who had access to Nelson's music and asked me to take care of it for her. One night, she invited me to dinner at a restaurant called Presto. They always used to eat out there as a couple. I got on with her quite well. Suddenly, I heard she had passed. I hadn't realised she was so ill."

Christopher Riddle:

"My father and I went to see the film *The French Connection* together, one of the few times Dad wasn't working on something. We went to the Wilshire Theatre on Santa Monica on Wilshire Boulevard. Dad was a big fan of Mel Brooks: *Silent Movie*, *High Anxiety*, and *Blazing Saddles* were some of his favourites.

"After Dad left the house in 1968, he had a beautiful apartment. He and I had been sharing the apartment as bachelors, and I looked after him, got his clothes laundered, etc. I thought we were set. He was dating his secretary, Naomi, at the time. I went out with them and brought a girlfriend to make up a four. We went to a favourite Italian restaurant of ours. After the meal, she went back to her mother's house in Beverly Hills. She lived at one end of the building, and her mother lived at the other end. I drove Dad back home and just as we did a right down Fountain Avenue, my father blurted out, 'I am going to marry Naomi.' He had only just got the divorce through from my mother, the interlocutory had just come through! I said to him straight, 'What for?' He said, 'I feel I owe it to her.' He and I had an honest exchange which ended with me saying, 'Shouldn't love come into it somewhere?

All the time Naomi had been scheming to separate him from his wife and family. He couldn't see it. I was 19 years going on 20 years. It was April 1970. They got married in his lawyer's backyard in Beverly Hills."

Naomi Riddle, née Tenenholtz, was the younger of two daughters born to Alex Tenenholtz and Ethel Fishman on March 8, 1921, in the state of New York. She was three months younger than Nelson. Her parents emigrated from the Russian town of Volkovitch to New York around the beginning of the twentieth century. Her father, Alex Elihu Tenenholtz, took up acting around 1906 in the Yiddish Theatre on New York City's lower east side. His stage name was Tenen Holtz. He quickly achieved fame with his work in New York Repertory Theatre. In the mid 1920's, Tenen Holtz moved his family to Hollywood after beginning to take minor roles in silent films. His credits include 46 silent and talking motion pictures from 1926 to 1939. Notable films were *Upstage* (1926), *Bringing Up Father* (1928), *Hollywood Hoodlum* (1934), and *Let Freedom Ring* (1939).

Tenen Holtz's work in the theatre gave Naomi early exposure to the stage and to the business which surrounded it. As a result, Naomi cultivated an appreciation for the performing arts which would play a powerful role in her life. She would go not only to see her father's performances, but to dozens of other productions in and around Los Angeles. After graduating from Los Angeles Fairfax High School in 1938, Naomi would spend some years working as a fashion model. During her years as a fashion model in the mid 1940's, Naomi met Dan Otto, a Los Angeles Art Centre School instructor.

Naomi met Nelson Riddle in 1954 while working on the television show *This Is Your Music*. He would later hire her as his full-time secretary around four years later.

During the mid-1960's, when Nelson's marriage to Doreen began to falter, Nelson sought comfort from Naomi during this turbulent period. On April 11, 1970, Naomi married Nelson in Los Angeles. Christopher Riddle was his father's best man and witnessed the wedding which took place at Nelson's lawyer's office.

Although only middle-aged, the mid-seventies saw Nelson's health begin to fail. He was treated for cirrhosis of the liver and kidney complications. This was to last for several years. To add to this, his marriage to Naomi was an unhappy union, so Nelson sought comfort with another and found a devoted and loving companion in Laurie Brooks.

Christopher Riddle: "My mother died in April 1980 at Cedars Sinai Hospital, and she wanted to be cremated and have her ashes scattered at sea by this society called Neptune Society. But my mother had changed her mind, and we all went out on a boat from San Pedro and scattered her ashes in the Pacific Ocean. Then we went back to have lunch at San Pedro Harbour. My father said there and then, 'I want that done for me,' but he didn't put that in writing. Guess what? His wishes were not carried out by Naomi and his ashes are inurned at Hollywood Forever which is situated right behind Paramount Pictures. There's a little crypt with the name Nelson Riddle. Fortunately, Naomi didn't have her ashes put there."

Nelson's death on 6th October 1985, at the comparatively young age of 64 years, was the result of a five-year battle against kidney and liver problems. The funeral that followed was naturally a very upsetting affair for his widow, Naomi, and the six Riddle children. The emotional turmoil was not helped by Naomi Riddle's attitude. For example, her stopping Frank Sinatra Jr.'s attendance at the funeral, saying, "If your father can't be bothered to attend, then you're not welcome..." This was devastating to the younger Frank who idolised Nelson and was attending in his own right, not as a deputy for his father.

Christopher Riddle: "Frank phoned me to say he wouldn't be attending Dad's funeral as he would be too upset and bereft of words to make any meaningful eulogy."

The heartfelt feelings that Sinatra had for Nelson is clearly shown in his letter to correspondent Charles Champlin of the Los Angeles Times:

FRANK SINATRA

December 10, 1985

Mr. Charles Champlin
Los Angeles Times
Times Mirror Square
Los Angeles, Calif.90053

Dear Chuck,

Please forgive me for being tardy with this letter, but with my traveling and the Holidays upon us I am just now catching up with my mail.

I completely agree with your thoughtful, well-researched piece about my good and dear friend Nelson Riddle that appeared in the TIMES, Oct.10. You're absolutely right -- my work was imbued with a warm, penetrating quality when Nelson came into my life. I can't tell you how much I'll treasure my memories of him and the work we did together.

I miss Nelson terribly; it saddens me so much to think the world is no longer blessed with his magnificent talent. And I miss him because he was my close friend and neighbor.

Nelson gave us so much to cherish and remember. I'm certain that whenever people want to listen to brilliance, whether they're sad, happy, celebrating or whatever, they'll invariably turn again and again to Nelson's work.

My good wishes for you always.

Warm regards,

Francis Albert

Letter from Frank Sinatra to the Los Angeles Times.
Courtesy of Rosemary Acerra's personal collection.

An emotional Linda Ronstadt gave a warm and glowing tribute to Nelson. Ella Fitzgerald was in attendance and would have given a eulogy but was disappointed as she wasn't asked to do so. The preceding period to the actual ceremony was marred as Nelson's children were summoned to a lawyer's office for the reading of the will and the subsequent knowledge that they had been disinherited. Nelson's widow, Naomi, would be the sole beneficiary.

Naomi died leaving her and her husband's estates to the University of Arizona.

9. WHAT'S NEW?

What's new?
Probably I'm boring you

In the late 70's, early 80's, Nelson was out of fashion with the singers of the day, except for one. She turned out to be the First Lady of Rock. I am sure the irony was not lost on Nelson when Linda Ronstadt first approached him.

Christopher Riddle: "I was listening to KNX Hollywood radio, a CBS station, one afternoon. There was an entertainment correspondent doing his daily report, and he said Linda Ronstadt had earned $15 million dollars in royalties. This would be around 1982. A week or so later, my father rang and said, 'Guess who I just spoke to? Linda Ronstadt. She asked if I would do a couple of arrangements, one of them for "Guess I'll Hang My Tears Out". I said, I'd love to do that, but I'd rather to do an album project.' Dad wasn't working at the time, so that was the right move!"

In more recent times, a number of international rock stars like Rod Stewart and Robbie Williams have released albums of songs from the *Great American Songbook*. Many of the songs they covered were Nelson Riddle arrangements and if not, were adapted from there. Rod Stewart acknowledged the status that Nelson holds in the history of American popular music. Many people considered these albums to be ground-breaking, yet twenty years earlier, a rock superstar of the time, Linda Ronstadt, had a music epiphany and wanted to resurrect the great songs and move them back to the top floor from their current basement level airing predominantly as elevator "Muzak".

Peter Asher, Linda's manager at the time, remembers how it all came about. Peter Asher CBE first burst on the pop music scene in the swinging sixties as part of the duo Peter and Gordon. They had a UK number one hit with "A World Without Love". Later, he forged a successful career in the US as a producer and manager.

I spoke to Peter at his office in Los Angeles:

"Linda was the first to do the standards, which had effectively become elevator music at the time. She defined her mission to get those songs out of the elevator, so she was the first pop star way ahead of Rod Stewart and Robbie Williams to record these songs. The general public were not listening to that sort of music, outside of the Sinatra, of course.

"She had a couple of goes, first with a piano and trio and a fellow songwriter, but it wasn't the right mixture. At the time, we thought would be a jazz trio style, but she was very much aware of Nelson's work, as was Linda's songwriter friend, John David Souther.

"We had a meeting with Nelson who we were both super impressed by and in awe of. We said to him, 'Would you write the arrangements for a couple of tunes for us for this planned project?' He said, 'No,' there was a short pause, then he said, 'but I will do an album.' He explained he wouldn't normally sign to arrange a couple of songs, but he would do a full album project, so Linda and I had no hesitation and said, 'Ok, let's do an album,' and that's how the project got off the ground.

"We had to inform our record company, and they were very disconcerted. I can't take the credit for saying the record would be a success, my role was as manager and producer; but I felt Linda had earned the right to make the records she wanted to make but did I think these recordings would outsell her previous albums fourfold? No. I would have certainly bet against. Those considerations should always be secondary anyway, as she needed to record from a musical perspective. She wanted to sing those songs, and it was my job to make that happen."

Linda Ronstadt: "I now realize I was taking a tremendous risk, and that Joe Smith (the head of Elektra Records, and strongly opposed) was looking out for himself and for me. When it became apparent I wouldn't change my mind, he said, 'I love Nelson so much! Can I please come to the sessions?' I said, 'Yes.' When the albums ... were successful, Joe congratulated me, and I never said, 'I told you so.'"

Linda Ronstadt and Nelson at ASCAP awards 1983. Photograph courtesy of The Nelson Riddle Music Library Arizona State University.

Linda Ronstadt's *Lush Life* went platinum 1984.
Photograph Elektra Records.

Peter Asher remembers:

"Initially, there was no airplay to speak of when these albums came out except perhaps for WNEW in New York by Jonathan Schwartz, I think. In terms of pop radio, there was nothing. Yet it was interesting as we got a lot of news stories about Linda that she had done it, as she was so successful and so famous; the fact she decided to do these songs, etc, and work with Nelson; the fact, of course, it was Nelson, and he was the best at what he did.

"After the record started to sell like crazy, we got another news-round of TV, etc, about it being an enormous hit, and it was outselling her rock and roll albums. Media attention came in waves, the first wave that she'd recorded the album and the second that it was a hit."

Nelson considered Linda Ronstadt to be one of the few rockers with the musicianship and voice to sing standard ballads.

Christopher Riddle: "My father said of Linda, 'She has a wonderful instrument, and I am going to teach her how to use it.'

"However, I didn't realise the terror Linda had put herself under. She wasn't used to singing with big orchestras and what that entailed. It was a whole new experience for her. My father and the piano player worked on things before she arrived, but it was terrible for her—like going in front of a firing squad. There were loads of re-takes. but the musicians were happy as they were remunerated accordingly!

"For example, on *Lush Life* the brass section wasn't needed until the afternoon, but someone messed up, and we were there all day and got paid for the whole day. It should have been only woodwind and strings for the morning. I played bass trombone on all three albums."

A number of Nelson's musicians felt the arrangements he did for Linda's three albums, although good, were not ground-breaking. He had broken that ground thirty years prior. He had nothing to prove to anybody. They may have missed the point. The three albums were hugely successful, the first two, *What's New?* and *Lush Life,* going platinum; the third, *For Sentimental Reasons,* went almost un-noticed, yet sold over one million records and went gold. Nelson earned more from his involvement on those three albums than anything he did in the Capitol years.

Commercial considerations aside, his albums with Linda were so important to him. He had been somewhat in the doldrums both musically and personally over the previous decade, so he was elated at being thrust back into the limelight. By his collaboration with Linda, he was introducing the Nelson Riddle sound to a new, younger audience.

Peter Asher didn't think a third album was a good idea, but Linda wanted to go ahead. Nobody knew how ill Nelson was at the time. It was a prophetic title in terms of why and when it was recorded. Nelson passed away on the 6th October 1985. Terry Woodson took over the baton of the Nelson Riddle Orchestra and concluded the recording of the third and final album for Linda Ronstadt.

Terry wrote the last arrangement on *For Sentimental Reasons*. Nelson used to sketch out his arrangements, but Terry having worked closely as the copyist for Nelson from 1980 to 1985, was able to decipher the correct notes. Terry couldn't write as well as Nelson, but he could interpret what he had written.

Sinatra had not been a fan of the albums Nelson did with Linda but may have been envious of the number of record sales, his only hit during the 80's coming from a stage show *New York, New York*. Nelson was approached around this time by Frank Military who was acting as go between saying Frank wanted to work with Nelson again. Nelson re-iterated his stance that "he would never work with that man ever again." He had never forgotten the perceived snub by Sinatra at his tribute dinner in 1978.

A week or so later, the phone rang at 6.30am. Nelson picked it up. "Nelson, it's Frank." The upshot of the conversation was that Sinatra wanted Nelson to be his musical director for the Reagan inauguration in 1985, like he had been for Kennedy's, back in 1961. Nelson was elated.

Ronald Reagan Inauguration 1985. Photograph courtesy
Christopher Riddle personal collection.

Christopher Riddle takes up the story:

"Frank had forgotten the time difference between them
and apologised to Dad for waking him. Dad replied that
it was ok he had to get up to answer the phone. I asked
him, 'What did Frank say?' Silence was Dad's reply.

"After the TV shows for the Reagan inauguration, Frank
threw a big party as only he could, the best of everything.
It was held at the Dolly Madison Ballroom at the
Madison Hotel in Washington. He had the whole
ballroom, naturally, and they had food stations all
around the perimeter. They would make you a meal,
whatever you wanted. It was always top notch with
Frank.

"He was waiting impatiently for Dad to arrive. They were chatting intensely for forty-five minutes or so, then Barbara, Frank's wife, came over and put her hand on his shoulder to try to get Frank to mingle. Frank said, 'Don't bother me, don't bother me.' My father was glowing. He was so pleased. That's when they started planning a new three CD recording of songs they had never done before, no repeat of any tunes, my father was thrilled. He didn't know it, of course, but he had barely nine months to live."

10. WHAT ARE YOU DOING THE
REST OF YOUR LIFE?

I want to see your face in every kind of light
In fields of gold and forests of the night

People will make their own minds up about the legacy that Nelson has left us. When we talk or write about legacy in general terms, it is not always possible for many people to leave an enduring legacy. With a true music legend like Nelson, his lasting legacy is secured, but perhaps the challenge is to maintain that legacy going forward. His living legacy has many different facets and can be heard and seen through many avenues: tangible, intangible, through new performances, repeat performances, through old recordings, through new recordings, in libraries and in concert theatres. It is nigh on impossible to pin it down.

We haven't established what Nelson liked to listen to, aside from the classical composers, of course; his interview with Jonathan Schwartz gave us some insight. Hearing one of his arrangements on radio or TV unexpectedly would give Nelson a buzz, and he fondly remembers hearing his arrangement of the old French nursery rhyme "Frere Jacques", translated to "Brother John" for recording purposes. Despite that, he never played his own music after it was completed and recorded, that was it. Playing classical music was his preference. His reading choices were in the main for biographies and history. For fictional narratives, he would turn his attention to Charles Dickens and Alexander Dumas.

Indeed, in 1984/85 with his health demonstrably failing, Nelson wanted to write a book on arranging music to pass on his unique knowledge and add to his legacy. He had been seeking a publisher for some time but despite his successful collaboration with Sinatra and latterly with Linda Ronstadt, his name wasn't that recognisable; not the household name it had been in the fifties and sixties. One young publishing executive had asked Nelson to "tell me what you have done". For all the writing Nelson had penned over the years, he was not a published author. Fortunately, help was at hand in the shape of Irene Kahn-Atkins, the daughter of the famous songwriter Gus Kahn, who did all the typing and re-writing. A published author herself, she tragically died before the book could be published. Nelson dedicated the book to her and his wife, Naomi, who he described as his best friend.

In this study guide, Nelson compares his approach to music to that of a journalist writing a story: "The facts are the important thing (in this case the musical ideas), and they have to be stated in as lean and economical a way as possible, since space and time are two very important factors."

Christopher Riddle: "*Arranged by Nelson Riddle* is our family's copyright. Dad put the finishing touches to that book when we were on a flight to New York. He was helped with finishing it by Irene Atkins. She's Lennie Atkins's wife. He was a fine musician, a violinist. He was the concertmaster on the Tommy Dorsey Band back when my father joined in 1944. Irene's father was Gus Kahn the famous songwriter. Irene helped my father put the book together, and I remember when we got off the plane in New York, she handed it to Frank Military of Warner, Chapple Music who went and published it. Lenny and I worked together when we were doing those recordings of Sinatra's, all those girls' names. After a session, we went to Sorrento's which is a restaurant just down the street from Warner Brothers. Anyhow, we were having dinner and in walks Frank who was with Gilly Russo. They sat down and joined us. Of course, the album never materialised although I believe some of the recordings are gathering dust somewhere in the label's vaults, who knows, one day? In the film *The Manchurian Candidate* they filmed some of it in Gilly's Russo's Restaurant, and Gilly has a cameo walk-on part."

Nelson's book required a project editor that understood the technical nature of the writing. Nelson was aided and abetted by the capable hands of Jeffrey Sultanoff. A publishing deal was obtained with Alfred Press and the book, *Arranged by Nelson Riddle – The Definitive Study of Arranging by America's No.1 Composer, Arranger and Conductor,* was published early in 1985. It was reported that it has sold in excess of 15,000 copies, for which is essentially a technical manual is a very respectable number.

There is a passage where he explains how he views vocalists as a featured instrument of the orchestra. Here is an excerpt:

"Male and female voices fall into four general categories. Those women with higher voices are classified as 'sopranos', those with lower voices 'altos'. The men having higher voices are called 'tenors', those with lower voices are designated 'basses'. Additionally, there are two subdivisions in these categories. Female voices slightly lower than the altos are called 'contraltos', and men whose voices are lower than tenors but higher than basses are called 'baritones'.

In writing for larger groups of voices, the contralto can be assigned to the alto parts, but is quite useful to give baritones their own line when scoring male voices, since the all-important root of a chord of any depth had best be assigned to a bass voice (or voices) to insure greater sonority and resonance.

In order to get better concept of the timbre and use of voices, it might be helpful to associate each of the various types of voices with the instruments in the orchestra they most resemble.

SOPRANOS are like flutes, trumpets or A violins.

ALTOS are like oboes, flugelhorns or B violins.

TENORS are like clarinets, French horns or violas.

BARITONES resemble bassoons, tenor trombones or celli.

BASSES are like contra bassoons, tubas or double string basses."

I know a number of young aspiring arrangers and composers who have purchased the book, many of which have, as a result, borrowed from Nelson. It is probably a fitting legacy for a man who had a low profile, in Hollywood terms at any rate, and would be content that his musical knowledge and arranging know-how was still being read and digested over thirty-five years after his death.

I spoke to my good friend Chris Walden who has been arranger for Michael Bublé, Michael Bolton, and many others. He also re-arranged John William's *Star Wars* for the Kennedy Center Honours awards, presented by US President Barack Obama.

Chris remembers:

"I first encountered Nelson Riddle from my own personal study of big-band arrangements. I majored at college in classical composition, but my preference was for big-band. I started playing in these bands when I was 18 years old. I always read credits from the Sinatra album and noted most of the orchestrations were by Nelson Riddle.

"I did a lot of take downs and studied his work. That way I learned a lot more about music writing. I have come to know a Riddle arrangement as soon as I hear the opening. He has his own identity which sets him apart from other arrangers like Billy May and Don Costa.

"He would also fully respect the lyrics and pay attention to them when he wrote an arrangement. An example is "You Make Me Feel So Young" where there is a reference to church bells ringing which Nelson replicates in his arrangement. It's not cheesy either. He does it in a subtle way. For the intro to "Pennies from Heaven" he has descending string line doubled up so you can actually visualise pennies falling from that sound.

"Speaking of his film music, there is a job definition called a music editor who works alongside the composer. After the music is recorded, the editor can cut the music as instructed. When I first came to Hollywood in the 1990's for my first film, an editor was assigned to me, his name was Rocky Moriana. He was an older guy, and he was Nelson's music editor in the 60's. He would always tell great stories about Nelson. Whilst Rocky was working with me, we would often have lunch at

Musso and Frank in Hollywood, and he told me that was Nelson's favourite restaurant, and we would always sit at Nelson's table. The waiters remembered Nelson. Rocky just adored Nelson. He mentioned him being very particular about his arrangements, and he said Nelson wasn't a pushover with directors. For example, if directors would make an unreasonable request to change the music, he would say they were wrong, and it needs to stay that way and why.

"I have often worked on projects that required Nelson's arrangements. For example, the Michael Bolton album *Sings Sinatra* done in 2000. I adapted Nelson's arrangements to make them my own, and also Michael Bolton sings in a higher register than Sinatra, so it was a case of transposing them to a different key."

Christopher Riddle: "As a complete side story and name drop, I was with a friend of mine attending a festival when I was introduced to film actor Dennis Quaid (*Independence Day, Wyatt Earp*). He had been performing with his band. He is extremely knowledgeable and personable. We spoke for some time as he was very interested in chatting about my father's work. He started out as a singer before acting, and he is a fine musician in his own right. It further illustrates the esteem with which my father is held not just in the music industry, but in the wider sphere of entertainment."

To illustrate Nelson's strong work ethic and arranging style, Norman Grantz, erstwhile producer for Ella Fitzgerald, commented at the time of Nelson's death in October 1985: "Of the top arrangers of his time, I think Nelson was the most serious. A lot of them would come in with the copyists literally trailing on behind them, doing a page at a time because the arranger had waited until the last minute. Not with Nelson. Everything under him was always laid out, yet you never felt locked in. You were always free."

An integral part of the Riddle legacy is for what he is renowned, writing arrangements for the world's top vocalists of the 20th century. I have covered in some depth the watershed orchestrations Nelson constructed for "Mona Lisa", "I've Got You Under My Skin" and "I've Got The World On a String". But I will highlight two more that I believe re-affirm Nelson's credentials as the foremost arranger of American popular music.

Peggy Lee's "The Folks Who Live On The Hill":

The "hook" in his orchestration for "The Folks Who Live On The Hill" is the restraint he shows. His sparse yet lush arrangement transports us gently into the story that Peggy Lee expertly conveys in the space provided by Nelson. Your imagination takes over, and you envisage the tale of every day delivered in the velvet tones of Lee's vocals. This recording is a perfect example of Nelson's Disney comparison as a musical imagineer.

Nelson's re-working of "All or Nothing at All" has to be the other ground-breaking orchestration that should be reviewed. Sinatra had recorded this song back in his early days with Harry James. The new arrangement came in 1966 when Nelson almost reluctantly agreed to do all but one of the arrangements for Sinatra's *Strangers in the Night* album. Mind you, close behind that in describing ground-breaking arrangements should be "Summer Wind" because of Nelson's ingenious use of the organ, never deployed before in an introduction to a Sinatra song. However, his milestone arrangement of "All or Nothing at All" is altogether something else. It fully transforms the song which was sung previously by Sinatra as a ballad standard into an up-tempo affair that gathers pace, ending in a crowning glory of musical orchestration. Try to listen to the live concert recording of this song. It's a real treat for Sinatra fans. I am sure Frank would venture a heavenly quote that "it's a gasser", and he is heard to confirm that at the end of the song by saying what a marvellous orchestration Nelson had produced. The array of different arrangements produced by Nelson for this album was almost as if he was saying, "I'll show you for giving me an album where I didn't arrange the title track" or perhaps as Skip Riddle was once told by his father, "Sometimes you have to have a smile on your face but a 'fuck you' in your heart!"

Christopher Riddle is the third born of Nelson Riddle's seven children, and the only one to become a professional musician. Christopher began his performing career at the age of six in a recording studio as a member of a junior vocal group that would go on to support immortals such as Frank Sinatra (on "High Hopes" and "Pocketful of Miracles"), Bing Crosby, Peggy Lee and Dean Martin.

At the age of nine, he formed the Riddle Combo, providing musical entertainment for private parties in Malibu, California, and its environs. After high school, he spent a year of study at the University of Southern California's School of Music. He then transferred to Trinity College at the Royal Academy in London and earned his BA (Hons) in performing arts.

Upon completion of his studies, Christopher decided to pursue a career within the big band orchestras. He served his apprenticeship as a bass trombonist in his father's orchestra but also gained valuable experience with the orchestras of Buddy Rich, Henry Mancini and Don Costa. Christopher has backed many of the greatest singers of the 20th century including Frank

Sinatra, Ella Fitzgerald, Sammy Davis Jr., and Linda Ronstadt.

Christopher by his own admission had become his father's shadow. He sought to accompany him on work assignments and eventually that would lead to him succeeding his father as leader of the NRO. It was a tough apprenticeship, however, as his father showed him no favours. It's a familiar story of a son having to be twice as good as any contemporary, and even if that is accomplished, don't expect any praise or encouragement. Nelson Riddle was not to prove an exception to the rule.

Christopher recalls:

"When I first joined the band at aged 19 years in 1969, my father insisted I kept my hair tidy (I had a Beatle mop at the time) if I was to play bass trombone in the Nelson Riddle Orchestra. He booked a barber's appointment for me at Sy Devore's in Hollywood. All the stars used to go there for a haircut and manicure. The first time I attended, there was comedian George Burns sitting in the chair. He had very little hair even then. To quote him directly, 'They had to send out a search party!' The barber was meticulous even so, taking great care and time, listening as we all were to the great man's anecdotes. After that, I made sure that I went at the same time every month in the hope that Mr. Burns ('call me George') was there. Another comedian I got to know very well from when we played on his TV show in Burbank was Jack Benny. He was so funny he didn't even have to say anything. His facial expressions were enough. I dated his daughter Joan for a while.

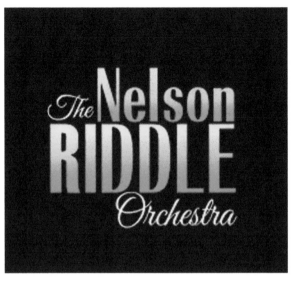

The NRO trademark. Photograph courtesy of Christopher Riddle.

Christopher Riddle conducts the NRO.
Photograph courtesy of Christopher Riddle.

Christopher Riddle continuing his father's legacy.
Photograph courtesy of Christopher Riddle.

Christopher Riddle and Tony Christie rehearsing London 2019.
Photograph courtesy of John Dawson Photographics.

CHRISTOPHER RIDDLE
Director of
The Nelson Riddle Orchestra

The Leader of The Pack. Photograph courtesy of Christopher Riddle.

"I made my debut for the NRO at 19 years. I had come back from my study in England. I had learned to drink beer and throw darts! I continued my study when arriving back in the USA with trombone teacher Robert Marsella. I was practising up to 5 hours a day.

"I was thrown in to see if I could swim. Kenny Shroyer gave up his chair for me. I had worked hard on my parts. Milt Bernhart and Tommy Shepherd helped me settle in. It wasn't easy; it wasn't a gimme.

"Even further down the line, Dad remained concerned about perceived nepotism. I remember once we were scoring a motion picture at Warner Bros. This was 1977. My second instrument was tuba. You were paid time and a half if you doubled up. I called the copyist to see if I needed to bring my tuba. I was assured it wasn't needed on this session. That was a relief because I had a two-seater Porsche at the time which I had restored, and I would rather have my girlfriend on the passenger seat than my tuba.

I left the tuba at home. When I got to the session, it was evident that a tuba would be needed. I don't think I was stitched up; however, my father read me the riot act in front of the whole band. Leave the tuba in the car at all times was his message, although he worded it slightly differently."

"That harsh introduction aside, there were many happy moments. For example in 1970, we were playing at Pick-Fair; it was a fascinating experience. This was at the estate owned by Douglas Fairbanks Snr and Mary Pickford, hence the name. I remember seeing a photograph of Lord Louis Mountbatten, Queen Elizabeth II's uncle, there. Apparently, he was a frequent visitor to the house. He was, of course, tragically assassinated by the Irish Republican Army (IRA) some years later."

"I remember we worked at Universal Pictures too. I walked along past Hitchcock Productions which is the next building before Universal. Being a great movie buff, I felt a shudder of pride walking in that very space that the great man had no doubt embraced. It was a great time as we were invited to many all-star parties. One such party I remember John Wayne and Ingrid Bergman attending. The company that did the catering was Chasens, famous for their catering and cocktails. This was manna from heaven for a young man making his way in the world. I got to know the maître d' at Chasens very well. He used to look after me. I have been very fortunate to have such marvellous life experiences, all down to my dad's status within the music industry."

"Later on in my career, I met two stalwart BBC radio 2 presenters in London, England. Alan Dell and Ray Moore both helped cement my father's legacy. Both were to become very good friends and very instrumental (no pun intended) in keeping my father's music alive. Both were avid Sinatra fans. Both are sadly no longer with us. My wife, Elizabeth, and I used to listen to Ray Moore's early morning show with hilarity. He was merciless in his wicked humour cracking jokes about Francis Albert Sinatra and his 'rug' as Ray called it. The origins of the hair used in the toupee Sinatra wore was the source of much amusement. Ray insisted it came from a woman's anatomy, and he wasn't shy in guessing which part. Enough said."

Ray Moore was a British broadcaster who was best known for hosting the early morning show on BBC Radio 2 between 1980 and 1988.

From 1980, until his last show on 28 January 1988, he hosted the early morning show on BBC Radio 2 developing an idiosyncratic broadcasting style which relied on a highly individual, gentle and sophisticated wit and repartee.

The regular exchange of banter established between Moore and Terry Wogan as the former handed over to the latter's breakfast show at 7:30 am became an established element of Radio 2's morning schedule.

Christopher Riddle: "Like I say Ray and his wife, Alma, became great friends. Ray was to attend our wedding and was even cracking jokes on the radio about this weird wedding he was going to!"

Another BBC radio 2 legend was Alan Dell. He mostly presented programmes of music from the dance band and swing eras. He was also an early presenter of *Pick of the Pops* in 1956 and, in his later years, of *Sounds Easy*, a Sunday afternoon programme on BBC Radio 2 which was notable for its attention to the recordings of Frank Sinatra and Peggy Lee (both of whom he pre-deceased) and Henry Mancini with the *Mancini Moment.* He won a 1983 Grammy Award in the Best Historical Album category for *The Tommy Dorsey/Frank Sinatra Sessions - Vols. 1, 2 & 3.*

Christopher continues: "Alan and I became great friends and he stood up for me at my wedding to Elizabeth which took place at Hammersmith Registry Office. Alan had been a longstanding champion of my father's music."

After Nelson's passing in 1985, Christopher was keen to lead the NRO and continue his father's legacy. The NRO was in demand, and he received a call from Willard Alexander Agency who were the biggest booker for big bands. They wanted to sign up the NRO and had several prestigious bookings lined up. However, Naomi Riddle had other ideas and refused to give Nelson's book of arrangements to Christopher. A month had passed since Nelson's death. Christopher had to earn a living. Naomi thought it was too soon.

Terry Woodson, who had taken over Vern Yocum's copyist business, helped Christopher out and told him to take what arrangements he needed. Christopher spent thousands of dollars getting the various orchestra parts copied and taped so they were "musician ready". Even so, when Naomi got wind of this, she threatened Christopher with legal action for using the Nelson Riddle Orchestra name!

Christopher, despite Naomi's best efforts, did establish himself as leader of the NRO and toured the USA extensively as well as numerous tours to the UK. It wasn't without unexpected difficulties as Christopher explains here:

"I was on the tour conducting the NRO with Louis Hoover in Birmingham UK, the Symphony Hall. This was in 2002. My drummer, Matt Skelton, said, 'I see you are back in April (2003). I hope I am going to be with the band.' I said, 'This is the first I've heard of this but certainly I want you, no question.' Matt is a marvellous drummer. I contacted my agent, Ted Schmidt, and he said he didn't know anything about it. Then I found out it was a guy called Greg Francis who was going to tour as the Nelson Riddle Orchestra UK! He actually played a couple of dates. I had to launch a lawsuit, and I used a guy called Ian Morse who was based in Manchester, the same law firm that had been used by the Glenn Miller Orchestra when he tried to pull the same thing on them. He didn't have any homework to do. He knew this guy and didn't like him a bit. He was onto him like a hound onto a hare.

"I launched the action in March 2003, and it lasted a year. By that time, I got a settlement because we were getting ready for the trial, and obviously, I was going to win. If I won, they would have to pay me everything that I had spent, damages or whatever. Ian Morse came to a settlement with them. The last time I sent money over was $25,000 which I borrowed against my house in Great Barrington, Massachusetts. I almost blinked before that, but I thought in for a penny, in for a pound. I had to stick it out. So, I did send the money, and Ian Morse contacted me about a week later and said they want to settle. I said how much? It was $52,000. I was in for over 100k. I said, 'Is this a pyrrhic victory?' He said, 'No because if you go to trial you will both be broke.' I now own the rights, and I just renewed them in 2013. They were trying to wait me out and get me to pack it in, but I had to stick it out. I was in for a total of $112,500. I had a meeting with my legal team at the Old Bailey. I had to wait to receive the settlement in April 2004.

"I saw Louis Hoover some years later on Queen Mary 2 in 2016, I think. It made me recall when we played the Royal Albert Hall when Louis didn't take me out with him to take a bow. He did two curtain calls without including me. He then said, 'You are coming to the after-show party, aren't you?' My answer? 'Fuck you, Louis.'"

More pleasant yet unusual experiences awaited Christopher:

"I was working with the band on the Regency Cruises back in 2005, a brand-new ship going from Malaga to Miami. First stop was Casablanca. It started out when the whole band met in Philadelphia. It was all a bit dodgy. They flew us from Philadelphia into Madrid. We had to run to make the connecting flight to Malaga by running a half mile sprint to the boarding gate. When we got down to Malaga, there were no instruments waiting for us, and none of our dress clothes. The very first night we did a show. Fortunately, everything turned up just in time, although the drummer's wife who was with us on tour had to borrow clothes for about three weeks as hers had gone astray, and her clothes caught up with her in Antigua.

"I have done a lot of big band crossings on QE2, and I also did the Saga Fjord in 1994 from Anchorage to Vancouver; those were Cunard ships. The captain got into trouble because he wanted to get us as close to a glacier as possible, and in doing so, he bent one of the propellers! We had a vibration all the way on the rest of the trip. It was a huge glacier; it went on for miles. That was the cruise Joan Fontaine and Jane Russell were on."

The Nelson Riddle Orchestra

New Theatre, Oxford, UK - Monday November 24th, 2008

Big band, swing and Sinatra came to the New Theatre tonight. Playing to an enthusiastic crowd, the Nelson Riddle Orchestra made its way through a series of classics such as "Route 66", "Lady is a tramp" and "I've Got You Under My Skin".

Nelson Riddle, an Academy Award winning composer and arranger, collaborated with the very best singers of the 40's and 50's including Frank Sinatra, Ella Fitzgerald and Nat King Cole. His orchestra is said to be the 'world's most recorded', due to its long establishment and collaborations with some of the greatest singers of the 20th century. His son, Christopher Riddle, now conducts and leads the orchestra in the same tradition and style set by his father.

Throughout this evening's performance, Riddle enjoyed light-hearted and easy banter with the audience, charming them with tales of his father and Frank, Ella and Nat. The Orchestra's crooner, Bryan Anthony, was equally charming in his banter, but where Riddle was disarming and sweet, Anthony was dashing and smooth.

Anthony has a full and powerful voice and belted out the tunes with ease and style akin to those who sang them the first time 'round. He has great stage presence and managed to get quite a few whoops and hollers from the audience, despite their ageing demographic.

The Orchestra itself was excellent, with some of the musicians impressively switching between instruments over the course of the evening, not to mention Riddle himself switching between conducting and playing the trombone. The band was highly professional and had a fantastic sound.

Much of the music has featured on movie soundtracks and television shows, and thus even for those of us who weren't around back then (a remarkably small proportion of the audience) it had a certain comforting familiarity about it, not to mention evoking images of swing dancing and parties in the 50's and 60's.

Overall it was a show that both the audience and the performers seemed to enjoy immensely, and should they be passing through a city near you on their 2008 UK tour, is definitely worth seeing.

Kate Bottriell, 25/11/08

How orchestra had audience on a string
By Hilary Porter

The Nelson Riddle Orchestra, Pavilion, Bournemouth

FRANK SINATRA called him "the greatest arranger in the world" and it is Nelson Riddle's incredible association with the crooner that is so spectacularly celebrated in this show.

What makes this unique concert so special is Riddle's son Christopher Riddle helping keep his father's musical legacy alive by leading his own 17-piece strong orchestra (and playing trombone) whilst telling a very personal story of his father's life in words, music and with projected images taken from the family album.

The visible resemblance to his father is uncanny and he conducts and leads the orchestra in the same tradition and style, using all the original charts and arrangements. Riddle's career spanned 50 years and helped establish artists like Nat King Cole and Ella Fitzgerald but his years with Sinatra, from 1953-62, were the golden age.

There could not have been a finer vocalist than Bryan Anthony to make our night with Ol' Blue Eyes more real. From the opening "I've Got the World on a String" he was the puppeteer who certainly had his audience on a string. Yet whilst he charmed us with his vocals on numbers like "I've Got You Under My Skin", "Night and Day" and "Witchcraft" our focus rarely shifted from this orchestra as a whole, demonstrating what a master of mood and subtlety Riddle was.

His ability was clearly demonstrated by this outstanding orchestra.

In recent years, the Radio Television Eire Concert Orchestra of Ireland included movements of *Cross-Country Suite* in its repertoire, performing Riddle's work in 2006 and 2007. In the 2007 concert, Christopher Riddle was conductor.

Christopher Riddle: "I did the Los Angeles Jazz Festival in 2010, and my sister Rosemary got in touch with Sue Raney, so I did some numbers with Sue and my 38-piece orchestra. We did some of the charts my father had written especially for her; in fact, some of them had been written for that BBC TV show back in 1964 called *The Best of Both Worlds* where Sue appeared with my father. One of the songs is called "I Stayed Too Long At The Fair". I had the score and the recording but there was something wrong. The score didn't match the recording I had. When I got out to Los Angeles, the harpist Gayle Levant, who was an old friend, worked with me on it, and we were able to fix it; otherwise, it would have been disastrous. Sue Raney adored my dad. She remembered me as I used to go and see her singing at a place called Dante's in the Valley. Sue had done TV variety type shows with Dad, and of course, she remembered me from the London show in 1964."

Christopher is always forward planning for the NRO, and moves are afoot for a new collaboration for touring UK and Europe although these plans have been put on hold due to the spread of the Covid-19 coronavirus. They are now scheduled to take place in 2021/22.

"I would like to go back to Australia with the band. My father did a world tour with Linda Ronstadt in 1984, and Sinatra toured there a lot, so we have a lot of connections there. I would like to play in front of the Australian public again."

"Similarly, I worked on Regent Cruises, like I said. They were so pleased I had just come back from England on the QE2 and had to fly from Kennedy Airport, New York to Los Angeles, because I was conducting the NR0 at the Beverly Wilshire Hotel for their richest world cruises. This was 2006."

New collaborations for NRO are envisaged, and they can take many forms. A number of pop artists started out their careers with big band in their hearts, but commercial considerations take precedent and the new wave of music in the late fifties and swinging (not musically speaking) sixties meant their big band dreams were left behind.

Tony Christie is a UK music legend. He started out singing with pop bands, working the tough northern club circuit. He then carved out a solo career in the 1960's garnering million seller hits like "Is This the Way to Amarillo", "Las Vegas", "I Did What I Did for Maria", "Avenues and Alleyways" (the theme to the hit TV series *The Protectors*) among many others. Pop music was not his first love, however.

I will let Tony take up the story:

"My dad was in the RAF, and he had this record collection. All big band stuff, Frank Sinatra. My heart was always in the music of the 30's and 40's. I often think I was born twenty years too late. I went into pop music because big band music was going out of business, but my ambition was to be a big band singer, but big band was dying out. In fact, one of the songs I want played at my funeral, but not yet though, is Peggy Lee's 'The Folks Who Live On The Hill'. I believe it is a Nelson Riddle arrangement. That is one of the best arrangements of all time. I had sung that song at a club in the sixties in a mining village. I had finished my normal set, and they wouldn't let me off the stage, and the only song I knew as an encore was the 'The Folks Who Live On The Hill' which I sang, accompanied only by my organ player. The crowd went berserk shouting, 'More, more, more.' To me, it's a husband-and-wife song, like myself married to my wife for fifty-odd years (not odd as in odd, but as in numbers), and it's a story song about the folks who live on the hill. I think it's probably the most romantic man and wife song ever written.

"If you think about 'I've Got You Under My Skin'. The arrangement changed the song, absolutely. People know that arrangement as soon as they hear the song; it's part of the song essentially. I have a rare record which Sinatra recorded in Australia. A fan who knew I was a Sinatra fan gave it to me. It was recorded at a live concert in the 50's."

How did Tony's association with the NRO come about? I first met Tony a few years ago when he kindly performed at a celebrity charity golf dinner I organised in memory of Perry Damone. We got talking about this music, that music, and he re-affirmed his love of the great standards and big band. I had known Christopher Riddle for a number of years, and we had kept in touch as he was looking to tour the UK and Europe again with the NRO. Normally, Christopher would have a resident male and female vocalist, not always a headline act. I wanted to facilitate something for Christopher, and at the same time it struck me how wonderful it would be for Tony to sing the great songs with the Nelson Riddle arrangements. My thoughts were to ask Sean Fitzgerald, Tony's son and manager, if that scenario would be of interest. Sean asked me to contact his dad direct, which I did. Suffice to say it was of great interest, something

Tony acknowledges in his autobiography *Tony Christie -The Song Interpreter.*

Similar discussions have been had with a number of American stars. Singing with the NRO is very much in demand. Gary Puckett of Gary Puckett and The Union Gap fame is another great vocalist due to tour the USA with the NRO. Further discussions have included other great voices such as film actors Robert Davi and Dennis Quaid. The message is clear, look out for an NRO date near you!

It is well chronicled the difficulties that Naomi Riddle posed in her dealings with Nelson's children, but it is to her credit in 1986 that with the help of Linda Ronstadt, she established the Nelson Riddle Memorial Library at Arizona State University. Linda had graduated from this university. The collection has thrived ever since, and I am grateful to them for providing a number of the images displayed herein. Perhaps Naomi had been playing the "gate-keeper" role she performed as Nelson's long employed secretary, and this was her final duty in securing Nelson's legacy in this everlasting memorial.

Rosemary Acerra: "Dad didn't fall into being a parent easily," she said. "He was an only child, and I don't think he was prepared to be in a big family. I think he did his best.... I miss his unique sense of humour."

Rosemary would bring each new album to Our Lady of Malibu Elementary School to impress her choir director, who was a nun. When Nelson Riddle saw his daughter with his *Sea of Dreams* album, which had on its cover a photo of a sexy, mermaid-like woman, he said, dryly, "You're not going to give Sister Mary Cora that album, are you?"

"He was crazy-busy — he was off doing concerts with Sinatra," she said. "When he was home for dinner, it was nice."

"I know that Dad compartmentalized things," she said. "When he was in music mode, you weren't going to interrupt him. But it was an amazing experience to be around."

Christopher Riddle: "The last two performances were when we were at the Hollywood Bowl with Ella Fitzgerald. Dad was too ill to do the rehearsal. He went to his dressing room and took a nap. Paul Smith, the piano player, stepped in and led the rehearsal."

"I said to my dad, 'What are we doing here? We have to be in New York in the morning.'

"He replied, 'I had to take the job. I couldn't let Ella down.'

"We went to New York the next day. We had a couple of rehearsals. It was a 55-piece orchestra, the venue was the South Street Seaport, and there was a barge there where we played, and that was his last performance."

The definition of the term legacy is "something left or handed down by a predecessor." In the case of Nelson Riddle, measuring and determining that "something" he left can be defined by his exquisite and selfless use of musical notes that put performers in the best possible place to showcase their talents. In most instances, they did just that.

11. HEY DIDDLE, RIDDLE

In celebration of NELSON RIDDLE'S centenary. One hundred questions.

No need to Google. The answers are at the back of the book.

1. What is Nelson's middle name?
2. What was the name of Nelson's father?
3. Which instrument did Nelson study before reverting to the trombone?
4. Name two of the classical French impressionists who were to greatly influence Nelson's arranging methodology.
5. Who was Nelson's mentor in Rumson, New Jersey, who recommended him to Tommy Dorsey?
6. What was the name of the conductor that was credited on the record label as arranger Nat "King" Cole's smash hit, *Mona Lisa*?
7. In 1959 Nelson arranged and conducted a five-album box set of songs and instrumentals celebrating the *George and Ira Gershwin Songbook* for which singer?
8. A gold record was awarded to Nelson for his no. 1 hit instrumental "Lisbon Antigua". In which movie was the song used, and who was the leading actor?
9. When asked whether he was feeling elated after completing the recording of "I've Got You Under My Skin", what was Nelson's response?
10. What was the first song that Nelson received a credit as arranger and conductor on the record label?

11. Sinatra and Riddle combined to produce a particular type of album where there was a theme throughout linking songs together. What is the name of that style of album?

12. What was the middle nickname of famed trumpeter Harry Edison?

13. Who starred in the first movie scored by Nelson in 1953?

14. The lyrics to theme song for the Howard Hawk's Movie *El Dorado* were borrowed from which famous poet?

15. How many instrumentals did Nelson compose for Ella Fitzgerald's five album set of the *George and Ira Gershwin Songbook*?

16. Which iconic Paris structure was featured in Nelson's composition sung by Frank Sinatra in the film *Paris When It Sizzles*?

17. Nelson had a hit record with the western theme "The Proud Ones". What was the central instrument used?

18. What organ of the body did actor Robert Stack refer to when giving a testimonial for Nelson Riddle's composition for the hit TV show *The Untouchables?*

19. Which building was described as "the house that Nat built"?

20. Who was the Grammy Award winning arranger that re-worked Nelson's arrangement of "Unforgettable" for Natalie Cole's duet with her father in 1990?

21. List the films Nelson was nominated for an Academy Award before eventually winning for *The Great Gatsby* in 1974.

22. After Nelson died in October 1985, who conducted the Nelson Riddle Orchestra for *For Sentimental Reasons,* the third album Nelson had arranged for Linda Ronstadt?

23. What was Nelson's reply when asked by Linda Ronstadt to write one or two arrangements for her?

24. How many times was Nelson nominated for an Academy Award (Oscar)?

25. *Our Town* resulted in an Emmy nomination for Nelson. Who won the Emmy Award for best song lyric?

26. When Frank Sinatra was a no-show at the tribute award ceremony for Nelson, who came to the rescue and saved the day?

27. What instrument did Nelson highlight in his arrangement for the memorable song "Love and Marriage"?

28. What was Nelson asked to do when Peter Lawford wrote to him following a Democratic party fundraiser for John F. Kennedy?

29. What did Frank Sinatra say when he first heard Nelson's arrangement of "I've Got the World on a String"?

30. What is the famous restaurant in Hollywood where Nelson and other celebrities dined on a regular basis?

31. What is the name of the town where Nelson spent his high school days studying music?

32. What instrument did Nelson liken Barbra Streisand's voice to?

33. What was the sensation Nelson felt when he first attended a concert where the orchestra played Ravel's "Bolero"?

34. Were Nelson and Frank Sinatra both members of the Tommy Dorsey Orchestra?

35. Where did Nelson learn to write for strings?

36. Mario Castelnuovo-Tedesco tutored Nelson in film score composition. From which country did he flee from the fascist uprising?

37. What is the name of the title theme to the Frank Sinatra western *Johnny Concho?*

38. What did Nat "King" Cole think Madison Avenue couldn't do?

39. Who co-starred with Frank Sinatra and Doris Day in *Young At Heart* and for whom wrote a tribute tune in a TV series ten years later?

40. How long did it take to produce Ella Fitzgerald's album *Sings The George and Ira Songbook?*

41. What position did Naomi Tenenholtz hold before becoming Nelson's second wife?

42. How did Peter Asher describe the status of the *Great American Songbook* at the start of Nelson collaboration with Linda Ronstadt?

43. In which US state is the Nelson Riddle Memorial Library?

44. What instrument became Nelson's instrument of choice after initially studying piano?

45. Which Irving Berlin song did Nelson adapt for his Oscar winning score of *The Great Gatsby* in 1974?

46. How old was Sue Raney when she made her debut album under Nelson's guidance?

47. What term did Rosemary use describing Nelson's role in producing arrangements for her that exactly tuned into her innermost feelings for each song?

48. What did Doris Day think of her participation with other cast members when starring in the *Pajama Game* movie?

49. What song did Eddie Fisher and Vic Damone record that Nelson arranged and conducted in a different way to suit each singer's vocal abilities?

50. Eddie Fisher's version was released as a single in 1966, reaching no. 2 on the Billboard easy listening charts. What was Fisher's immediate reward?

51. From what film did the song "A Day in the Life of a Fool" originate from?

52. Nelson's son Christopher chose to follow his father and study the trombone as his favoured instrument. What was his second instrument?

53. To whom did Nelson lose out on the Oscar for best score for a musical film in 1961 for *Can Can,* and what was the name of the winning film?

54. There was an A-to-Z medley of songs that Nelson devised for the Sinatra TV special birthday tribute in 1983. Sung as a duet by Steve Lawrence and Vic Damone, which song qualified as "X" in the twenty-six song medley?

55. Julie Andrews described Nelson as *Eye-ore,* a character from which book?

56. What did Nelson forget to do when carrying out a very complicated procedure trying to synchronise orchestral backing to Sinatra's previously recorded rhythm section, and what was Sinatra's response?

57. When Sinatra started to plan a new album with Nelson, he would invariably discuss various classical composers to the point that after a couple of hours Nelson was having to reach for the headache tablets. What, after those long and intense conversations, did Sinatra say about the rest of the album?

58. How did Peter Lawford refer to a period of reflection in his letter to Nelson requesting Nelson waive his right to royalties for any future broadcasts of the JFK fundraising concerts?

59. Who replaced the banished Peter Lawford and was cast as Alan-A-Dale in the film *Robin and the 7 Hoods*?

60. Nelson's *Cross-Country Suite* was the recipient of one of the first Grammy Awards. Who was the featured clarinettist on the album?

61. Nelson worked with two of the world's finest violinists for a boxed set album released in 1981. One of them was French jazz violinist Stephane Grappelli. Who was the other?

62. What was the date and location of Nelson's final concert?

63. Chris Walden refers to his association with Rocky Moriana with whom Nelson had worked many times as film editor on various movies. Chris and Rocky used to visit Nelson's favourite restaurant and sit on his favourite table. What is the name of this famous restaurant in Hollywood?

64. When Nelson was commissioned as musical director for the 78th Annual Academy Awards (Oscars), what request was made of Christopher Riddle by "fixer" Johnny Fresco?

65. When rehearsing for Sinatra's retirement concert, Christopher's music sheets were jettisoned by a flourish of Nelson's baton into the lap of which Hollywood actor?

66. When visiting London for a film premiere of *What A Way to Go* in 1964, Nelson and his family were invited to which famous war time politician's residence?

67. Back in 1953 when Capitol Records decided they wanted a new style and music direction for Sinatra, Nelson metaphorically referred to taking on a new profession. Was it Tinker, Tailor, Soldier or Spy?

68. Where was Nelson born and in which state?

69. When writing arrangements, Nelson would refer to the tempo being like what part of the human body's function?

70. What award was Nelson nominated for top music director for the romantic comedy *Merry Andrew* starring Danny Kaye and Pier Angeli?

71. The score of *L'il Abner* was another Oscar nomination for Nelson, but he lost out to André Previn for which film?

72. Nelson wrote the hit tune called "Lolita Ya Ya", and it was implied that the banal lyrics for that song were Nelson's attempt to get his own back, on whom or what?

73. With whom did Nelson share the orchestration duties with for the film biopic *Harlow* released in 1965?

74. In which film did Nelson compose the tune "Kiss Me Pumpkin", an up-tempo number designed to add a sleazy feel to the central character's numerous sexual encounters?

75. What character should Nelson play if he had a part in the movie *Batman*?

76. Name the title of the theme Nelson wrote for the TV movie starring William Holden who played a veteran cop working the last day before his retirement?

77. Where is the Oscar statuette kept which Nelson won for Best Score for a Motion Picture for *The Great Gatsby* in 1974?

78. What was the last film for which Nelson wrote the score?

79. What money related gift did Rosemary Clooney give to Nelson and what did the inscription say?

80. Peter Asher, Linda Ronstadt's manager and producer, was part of a pop duet in 1960's called Peter and Gordon. What was the name of their UK no. 1 chart hit?

81. What did Linda Ronstadt say to Frank Sinatra during her concert when she noticed him sat in the audience?

82. Why did Christopher Riddle leave his tuba at home when travelling to play in his father's orchestra for a motion picture Nelson was scoring for Warner Bros? There are two correct answers, either one will do but you get a bonus point if you get both.

83. Known as "The King of Bolero", with whom did Nelson record the single "Mexicali Rose"?

84. *Yes............* was an album collaboration with Dinah Shore in 1958. Fill in the blank to complete the title.

85. When Nelson put together the A-Z medley for *Sinatra's TV All Star Party* in 1983, Sinatra joined Vic Damone and Steve Lawrence for the final chorus of which song?

86. Name the Nat "King" Cole tribute instrumental album Nelson recorded one year after Cole's death?

87. What was the nickname Nelson gave to Screen Gems, and when Christopher visited their offices, what was unusual about the chocolates they offered to guests? Half a point for each correct answer.

88. What was the type of music that Nelson used in his arrangement of the promo disc by film actress Yvonne De Carlo titled *Take it or Leave It?*

89. What was the name of the producer who engaged Nelson's services for the TV series *Emergency* and *Project UFO?*

90. Barbra Streisand asked that Paramount employ Nelson Riddle to be one of the orchestrators for *Funny Girl.* This was Streisand's film debut and there were numerous rumours of unrest among other cast members who had their roles diminished at the behest of Streisand. What did director William Wyler reply when asked if working with Streisand had proved difficult?

91. Judy Garland visited the Riddle household and left something behind, what was it?

92. The film *Can Can* was released in 1960 and saw Nelson nominated for an Oscar once again. A famous Cole Porter song was left out of the film. What was the name of the song? Nelson compensated somewhat for the producer's omission; how did he achieve that?

93. For the Sinatra album *Strangers in The Night,* Nelson used an instrument for the introduction in "Summer Wind" that hitherto had not been used to introduce a Sinatra song. What was the instrument used?

94. What would never end "Without a Song"?

95. Nelson was involved with Stanley Kramer's film about Doctor T. How many fingers did the doctor have?

96. Shirley Bassey combined with Nelson to record a number 5 hit in the early 60's. Later on in her career, this song was to become an important part of Bassey's live concerts. Name the song.

97. What time of day did Sinatra prefer to record and why?

98. What song does Tony Christie describe as the best husband and wife song ever written?

99. In later years, Nelson felt his music was better appreciated in the UK and one other country than in his native USA. What was the other country?

100. Although very ill, Nelson travelled overnight from Los Angeles to perform his last gig with a 55-piece orchestra at South Street Seaport in New York. This was an exhausting schedule but when asked by Christopher Riddle why he had committed to play in L.A only the night before, what was his reply?

Thanks and Acknowledgements:

Rosemary Acerra
Bryan Anthony
Peter Asher CBE
Stan Britt
Charles Champlin
Tony Christie
Pete Christlieb
John Dawson
Sean Fitzgerald
Gary Littlefield
Johnny Mathis
Jimmy Maxwell
John S. Miller
Vinesh Patel
Gary Puckett
Sue Raney
James Robinson
Linda Ronstadt
Nelson "Skip" Riddle III
Jonathan Schwartz
Robert Scott
Frank Sinclair
David Smith
Trish Stevens
Joe Francis Sutkowski
Chris Walden
David Ward
Terry Woodson

Special thanks to performers past and present

Discography

Albums

- *The Music From "Oklahoma!" (Capitol, 1955)*
- *Lisbon Antigua* (1956)
- *The Tender Touch* (Capitol, 1956)
- *Hey...Let Yourself Go!* (Capitol, 1957)
- *C'mon... Get Happy!* (Capitol, 1958)
- *Sea of Dreams* (Capitol, 1958)
- *Witchcraft!* (1958)
- *Sing a Song with Riddle* (Capitol, 1959)
- *The Joy of Living* (Capitol, 1959)
- *Dance To The Music Of "Tenderloin"* (Capitol, 1961)
- *Magic Moments from "The Gay Life"* (Capitol, 1961)
- *Love Tide* (Capitol, 1961)
- *Love Is a Game of Poker* (Capitol, 1962)
- *Route 66 Theme and Other Great TV Hits* (Capitol, 1962)
- *White on White, Shangri-La, Charade & Other Hits of 1964* (Reprise, 1964)

- *Hits of 1964* (Reprise, 1964)
- *Original Music From "The Rogues"* (RCA, 1964)
- *Interprets Great Music, Great Films, Great Sounds* (Reprise, 1964)
- *NAT: An Orchestral Portrait of Nat "King" Cole* (Reprise, 1966)
- *Music for Wives and Lovers* (United Artists, 1967)
- *The Bright and the Beautiful* (Liberty, 1967)
- *The Riddle of Today* (Liberty, 1968)
- *The Contemporary Sound of Nelson Riddle* (United Artists, 1968)
- *British Columbia Suite* (Capilano, 1969)
- *The Look of Love* (Bulldog, 1970)
- *Nelson Riddle Conducts the 101 Strings* (Marble Arch, 1970)
- *The Sound of Magnificence with 101 Strings* (Alshire, 1970)
- *Changing Colors* (MPS, 1972)
- *Communication* (MPS, 1972)
- *Vive Legrand!* (Daybreak, 1973)
- *Top Hat* (Angel, 1981)
- *Romance Fire and Fancy* (Intersound, 1983)

With Nat "King" Cole

- *Unforgettable* (Capitol, 1954)
- *Nat King Cole Sings for Two in Love* (Capitol, 1954)
- *The Piano Style of Nat King Cole* (Capitol, 1955)

- *Ballads of the Day* (Capitol, 1956)
- *This is Nat King Cole* (Capitol, 1957)
- *St. Louis Blues* (Capitol, 1958)
- *Cole Español* (1958)
- *To Whom It May Concern* (Capitol, 1959)
- *Wild Is Love* (Capitol, 1960)
- *Nat Cole Sings the Great Songs* (Capitol, 1964)

With Ella Fitzgerald

- *Ella Fitzgerald Sings the George and Ira Gershwin Songbook* (Verve, 1959)
- *Ella Swings Gently with Nelson* (Verve, 1962)
- *Ella Swings Brightly with Nelson* (Verve, 1962)
- *Ella Fitzgerald Sings the Jerome Kern Songbook* (Verve, 1963)
- *Ella Fitzgerald Sings the Johnny Mercer Songbook* (Verve, 1964)
- *Ella Loves Cole*
- *Dream Dancing* (Atlantic, 1972)
- *The Best Is Yet to Come*(Pablo, 1982)

With Linda Ronstadt

- *What's New?* (Elektra, 1983)
- *Lush Life* (Elektra, 1984)
- *For Sentimental Reasons* (Elektra, 1986)

With Frank Sinatra

- *Swing Easy* (Capitol, 1954)
- *Songs for Young Lovers* (Capitol, 1954)

- *In the Wee Small Hours* (Capitol, 1955)
- *Songs for Swingin' Lovers* (Capitol, 1956)
- *This is Sinatra* (Capitol, 1956)
- *Close to You* (Capitol, 1956)
- *A Swingin' Affair!* (Capitol, 1956)
- *This is Sinatra (Volume 2)* (Capitol, 1958)
- *Frank Sinatra Sings for Only the Lonely* (Capitol, 1958)
- *Look to Your Heart* (Capitol, 1959)
- *Nice 'n' Easy* (Capitol, 1960)
- *Sinatra's Swingin' Session!!!* (Capitol, 1960)
- *All the Way* (Capitol, 1961)
- *Sinatra Sings of Love & Things* (Capitol, 1962)
- *The Concert Sinatra* (1963)
- *Sinatra's Sinatra* (1963)
- *Days of Wine & Roses* (Reprise, 1964)
- *Strangers in the Night* (Reprise, 1966)
- *Moonlight Sinatra* (Reprise, 1966)

With Keely Smith

- *I Wish You Love* (Capitol, 1958)
- *Swingin' Pretty* (Capitol, 1959)
- *Little Girl Blue/Little Girl New* (Reprise, 1963)

With others(alphabetically):

- Anna Maria Alberghetti, *Warm and Willing* (Capitol, 1960)
- Shirley Bassey, *Let's Face the Music* (Columbia, 1962)

- Shirley Bassey, *Shirley Bassey Sings the Hit Song from Oliver!* (United Artists, 1963)
- Rosemary Clooney, *Rosie Solves the Swingin' Riddle* (RCA Victor, 1961)
- Rosemary Clooney, *Love* (Reprise, 1962)
- Bing Crosby, *Return to Paradise Islands* (Reprise, 1964)
- Sammy Davis Jr., *That's Entertainment* (MGM, 1974)
- Frank Sinatra Jr., *Spice* (Daybreak, 1971)
- Buddy DeFranco, *Cross Country Suite* (Dot, 1958)
- Eddie Fisher, *Games That Lovers Play* (RCA, 1966)
- Judy Garland, *Judy* (1956)
- Judy Garland, *Judy in Love* (Capitol, 1958)
- Antonio Carlos Jobim *The Wonderful World of Antonio Carlos Jobim* (Warner Bros, 1965)
- Jack Jones *There's Love and There's Love and There's Love* (Kapp, 1965)
- Kiri Te Kanawa, *Blue Skies* (London, 1985)
- Steve Lawrence, *Portrait of Steve* (MGM, 1972)
- Peggy Lee, *The Man I Love* (Capitol, 1957)
- Peggy Lee, *Jump for Joy* (Capitol, 1958)
- Dean Martin, *This Time I'm Swingin'* (Capitol, 1960)
- Dean Martin, *Cha Cha de Amor* (Capitol, 1962)
- Johnny Mathis, *I'll Buy You a Star* (Capitol, 1962)
- Johnny Mathis, *Live it Up* (Columbia, 1963)
- Oscar Peterson, *Oscar Peterson & Nelson Riddle* (Verve, 1964)

- Sue Raney, *When Your Lover Has Gone* (Capitol, 1958)
- Mavis Rivers, *Take a Number* (Capitol, 1959)
- Tommy Sands, *When I'm Thinking of You* (Capitol, 1959)
- Tommy Sands, *Dream with Me* (Capitol, 1960)
- Dinah Shore, *Dinah, Yes Indeed!* (Capitol, 1959)
- Phil Silvers, *Phil Silvers and Swinging Brass* (Columbia, 1956)
- Frank Sinatra Jr., *His Way* (Daybreak, 1972)
- Ed Townsend, *New in Town* (Capitol, 1959)
- Ed Townsend, *Glad to Be Here* (Capitol, 1959)
- Slim Whitman, *All Time Favorites* (1964)
- Danny Williams, *Swinging for You* (1962)

Singles

- "Lisbon Antigua" (US No. 1 - February 1956)
- "Port Au Prince" (US No. 20 - April 1956)
- "Theme from The Proud Ones" (US No. 39 - July 1956)
- "Route 66 Theme" (US No. 30 - June 1962 - AC No. 9, 1962)
- "Naked City Theme" (US No. 130 - October 1962)
- "What's New" (Featuring Linda Ronstadt) (US No. 53 - December 1983 - AC No. 5, 1983)
- "I've Got a Crush On You" (Featuring Linda Ronstadt) (AC No. 7, 1984)

Sources: Billboard Top Pop Singles, Billboard Adult Contemporary Billboard Bubbling Under Singles Books

Arranger for film and television

- *The Rosemary Clooney Show* (1956)
- *Pal Joey* (1957)
- *Can-Can* (1960)
- *Robin and the 7 Hoods* (1964)
- *Paint Your Wagon* (1969)
- *On a Clear Day You Can See Forever* (1970)
- *The Julie Andrews Hour* (1973)
- *The Carpenters: Music, Music, Music* (1980)
- *Till There Was You*
- *A Man and His Music*

Composer for film and television

- *Lisbon* (1956))
- *The Girl Most Likely* (1957)
- *Li'l Abner* (1959)
- *The Untouchables* (1959 TV)
- *Route 66* (1960 TV)
- *Naked City* (1960 TV)
- *Ocean's Eleven* (1960)
- *Lolita* (1962)
- *4 for Texas* (1963)
- *The Rogues (TV series)* (1964)
- *A Rage to Live* (1965)
- *Batman* (1966 film)
- *Batman* (1966–68 TV)
- *El Dorado* (1967)
- *How to Succeed in Business Without Really Trying* (1967)

- *This Is Your Life* (1971)
- *Emergency!* (1972)
- *The Great Gatsby* (1974)

Source: www.discogs.com

Answers (with questions) to the centenary quiz:

1. What is Nelson's middle name? SMOCK.
2. What was the name of Nelson's father? NELSON RIDDLE.
3. Which instrument did Nelson study before reverting to the trombone? PIANO.
4. Name two of the classical French impressionists who were to greatly influence Nelson's arranging methodology? RAVEL AND DEBUSSY.
5. Who was Nelson's mentor in Rumson, New Jersey, who recommended him to Tommy Dorsey? BILL FINEGAN.
6. What was the name of the conductor that was credited on the record label as arranger Nat "King" Cole's smash hit, "Mona Lisa"? LES BAXTER.
7. In 1959 Nelson arranged and conducted a five-album box set of songs and instrumentals celebrating the *George and Ira Gershwin Songbook* for which singer? ELLA FITZGERALD.
8. A gold record was awarded to Nelson for his no. 1 hit instrumental "Lisbon Antigua". In which movie was the song used, and who was the leading actor? LISBON STARRING RAY MILLAND.
9. When asked whether he was feeling elated after completing the recording of "I've Got You Under My Skin", what was Nelson's response? THAT HE WAS RELIEVED TO HAVE FINISHED IT IN TIME.
10. What was the first song that Nelson received a credit as arranger and conductor on the record label? UNFORGETTABLE.

11. Sinatra and Riddle combined to produce a particular type of album where there was a theme throughout linking songs together. What is the name of that style of album? A CONCEPT ALBUM.

12. What was the middle nickname of famed trumpeter Harry Edison? SWEETS.

13. Who starred in the first movie scored by Nelson 1953? MICKEY ROONEY.

14. The lyrics to theme song for the Howard Hawk's movie *El Dorado* were borrowed from which famous poet? EDGAR ALLAN POE.

15. How many instrumentals did Nelson compose for Ella Fitzgerald's five album set of the *George and Ira Gershwin songbook*? SIX.

16. Which iconic Paris structure was featured in Nelson's composition sung by Frank Sinatra in the film *Paris When It Sizzles*? THE EIFFEL TOWER.

17. Nelson had a hit record with the western theme "The Proud Ones". What was the central instrument used? A WHISTLING VOCAL.

18. What organ of the body did actor Robert Stack refer to when giving a testimonial for Nelson Riddle's composition for the hit TV show *The Untouchables?* THE HEART.

19. Which building was described as "the house that Nat built"? CAPITOL RECORDS TOWER ON HOLLYWOOD AND VINE.

20. Who was the Grammy Award winning arranger that re-worked Nelson's arrangement of "Unforgettable" for Natalie Cole's duet with her father in 1990? JOHNNY MANDEL.

21. List the films Nelson was nominated for an Academy award before eventually winning for *The Great Gatsby* in 1974. L'IL ABNER, CAN CAN, ROBIN AND 7 HOODS, PAINT YOUR WAGON.

22. After Nelson died in October 1985, who conducted the Nelson Riddle Orchestra for *For Sentimental*

Reasons, the third album Nelson had arranged for Linda Ronstadt? TERRY WOODSON.

23. What was Nelson's reply when asked by Linda Ronstadt to write one or two arrangements for her? HE REFUSED BUT SAID HE WOULD DO AN ALBUM.

24. How many times was Nelson nominated for an Academy Award (Oscar)? FIVE.

25. *Our Town* resulted in an Emmy nomination for Nelson. Who won the Emmy award for best song lyric? SAMMY CAHN.

26. When Frank Sinatra was a no-show at the tribute award ceremony for Nelson, who came to the rescue and saved the day? GREGORY PECK.

27. What instrument did Nelson highlight in his arrangement for the memorable song "Love and Marriage"? TUBA.

28. What was Nelson asked to do when Peter Lawford wrote to him following a Democratic party fundraiser for John F. Kennedy? WAIVE HIS ROYALTIES.

29. What did Frank Sinatra say when he first heard Nelson's arrangement of "I've Got the World on a String"? THAT'S A GASSER. WHO DID THAT?

30. What is the famous restaurant in Hollywood where Nelson and other celebrities dined on a regular basis? MUSSO AND FRANK.

31. What is the name of the town where Nelson spent his high school days studying music? RUMSON, NEW JERSEY.

32. What instrument did Nelson liken Barbra Streisand's voice to? AN OBOE.

33. What was the sensation Nelson felt when he first attended a concert where the orchestra played Ravel's "Bolero"? BEING SLAPPED IN THE FACE.

34. Were Nelson and Frank Sinatra both members of the Tommy Dorsey Orchestra? YES, BUT NOT AT THE SAME TIME.
35. Where did Nelson learn to write for strings? IN THE MERCHANT MARINE.
36. Mario Castelnuovo-Tedesco tutored Nelson in film score composition. From which country did he flee from the fascist uprising? ITALY.
37. What is the name of the title theme to the Frank Sinatra western *Johnny Concho?* WAIT FOR ME.
38. What did Nat "King" Cole think Madison Avenue couldn't do? SEE IN THE DARK.
39. Who co-starred with Frank Sinatra and Doris Day in *Young At Heart* and for whom wrote a tribute tune in a TV series ten years later? GIG YOUNG.
40. How long did it take to produce Ella Fitzgerald's album *Sings The George and Ira Songbook?* EIGHT MONTHS.
41. What position did Naomi Tenenholtz hold before becoming Nelson's second wife? HIS SECRETARY.
42. How did Peter Asher describe the status of the *Great American Songbook* at the start of Nelson collaboration with Linda Ronstadt? AS ELEVATOR MUSIC.
43. In which US state is the Nelson Riddle Memorial Library? ARIZONA.
44. What instrument became Nelson's instrument of choice after initially studying piano? TROMBONE.
45. Which Irving Berlin song did Nelson adapt for his Oscar winning score of *The Great Gatsby* in 1974? WHAT I'LL DO.
46. How old was Sue Raney when she made her debut album under Nelson's guidance? SEVENTEEN.
47. What term did Rosemary use describing Nelson's role in producing arrangements for her that tuned exactly into her innermost feelings for each song? ENNOBLED

48. What did Doris Day think of her participation with other cast members when starring in the *Pajama Game* movie? THAT SHE NEEDED TO BECOME A PART OF A WELL-OILED MACHINE.

49. What song did Eddie Fisher and Vic Damone record that Nelson arranged and conducted in a different way to suit each singer's vocal abilities? GAMES THAT LOVERS PLAY.

50. Eddie Fisher's version was released as a single in 1966, reaching no. 2 on the Billboard easy listening charts. What was Fisher's immediate reward? A RECORD CONTRACT.

51. From what film did the song *A Day in the Life of a Fool* originate from? BLACK ORPHEUS.

52. Nelson's son Christopher chose to follow his father and study the trombone as his favoured instrument. What was his second instrument? TUBA.

53. To whom did Nelson lose out on the Oscar for best score for a musical film to in 1961 for *Can Can*, and what was the name of the winning film? ANDRE PREVIN. WEST SIDE STORY.

54. There was an A-to-Z medley of songs that Nelson devised for the Sinatra TV special birthday tribute in 1983. Sung as a duet by Steve Lawrence and Vic Damone which song qualified as "X" in the twenty-six song medley? EXACTLY LIKE YOU.

55. Julie Andrews described Nelson as *Eye-ore,* a character from which book? WINNIE THE POOH.

56. What did Nelson forget to do when carrying out a very complicated procedure trying to synchronize orchestral backing to Sinatra's previously recorded rhythm section, and what was Sinatra's response? TO TUNE SINATRA'S VOICE TO THE MUSIC. SINATRA GAVE HIM A SECOND CHANCE.

57. When Sinatra started to plan a new album with Nelson, he would invariably discuss various

classical composers to the point that after a couple of hours Nelson was having to reach for the headache tablets. What, after those long and intense conversations, did Sinatra say about the rest of the album? "NELSON, DO WHAT YOU THINK IS BEST."

58. How did Peter Lawford refer to a period of reflection in his letter to Nelson requesting Nelson waive his right to royalties for any future broadcasts of the JFK fundraising concerts? THERE WILL NOW BE A TEN MINUTE INTERLUDE.

59. Who replaced the banished Peter Lawford and was cast as Alan-A-Dale in the film *Robin and the 7 Hoods*? BING CROSBY.

60. Nelson's *Cross-Country Suite* was the recipient of one of the first Grammy Awards. Who was the featured clarinettist on the album? BUDDY DE FRANCO.

61. Nelson worked with two of the world's finest violinists for a boxed set album released in 1981. One of them was French jazz violinist Stephane Grappelli; who was the other? YEHUDI MENUHIN.

62. What was the date and location of Nelson's final concert? SOUTH STREET SEAPORT, BROOKLYN, NEW YORK.

63. Chris Walden refers to his association with Rocky Moriana with whom Nelson had worked many times as film editor on various movies. Chris and Rocky used to visit Nelson's favourite restaurant and sit on his favourite table. What is the name of this famous restaurant in Hollywood? MUSSO AND FRANK.

64. When Nelson was commissioned as musical director for the 78th Annual Academy Awards (Oscars), what request was made of Christopher Riddle by "fixer" Johnny Fresco? TO LOG WHERE THE NEEDLE DROPS COME IN.

65. When rehearsing for Sinatra's retirement concert, Christopher's music sheets were jettisoned by a flourish of Nelson's baton into the lap of which Hollywood actor? EDWARD G. ROBINSON.

66. When visiting London for a film premiere of *What A Way to Go* in 1964, Nelson and his family were invited to which famous war time politician's residence? WINSTON CHURCHILL.

67. Back in 1953 when Capitol Records decided they wanted a new style and music direction for Sinatra, Nelson metaphorically referred to taking on a new profession. Was it Tinker, Tailor, Soldier or Spy? TAILOR.

68. Where was Nelson born and in which state? HAVENSACK, NEW JERSEY.

69. When writing arrangements, Nelson would refer to the tempo being like what part of the human body's function? HEART.

70. What award was Nelson nominated for top music director for the romantic comedy *Merry Andrew* starring Danny Kaye and Pier Angeli? GOLDEN LAUREL AWARD.

71. The score of *L'il Abner* was another Oscar nomination for Nelson, but he lost out to André Previn for which film? PORGY AND BESS.

72. Nelson wrote the hit tune called "Lolita Ya Ya", and it was implied that the banal lyrics for that song were Nelson's attempt to get his own back on whom or what? ROCK AND ROLL.

73. With whom did Nelson share the orchestration duties with for the film biopic *Harlow* released in 1965? AL HAM.

74. In which film did Nelson compose the tune "Kiss Me Pumpkin", an up-tempo number designed to add a sleazy feel to the central character's numerous sexual encounters? RAGE TO LIVE.

75. What character should Nelson play if he had a part in the movie *Batman*? THE RIDDLER.

76. Name the title of the theme Nelson wrote for the TV movie starring William Holden who played a veteran cop working the last day before his retirement? THE BLUE KNIGHT.

77. Where is the Oscar statuette kept which Nelson won for Best Score for a Motion Picture for *The Great Gatsby* in 1974? NELSON RIDDLE MEMORIAL LIBRARY, ARIZONA STATE UNIVERSITY.

78. What was the last film for which Nelson wrote the score? CHATTANOOGA CHOO CHOO.

79. What money related gift did Rosemary Clooney give to Nelson, and what did the inscription say? A GOLD MONEY CLIP INSCRIBED, "WHEN YOU LOSE A TWENTY DOLLAR BILL AGAIN YOU WILL HEAR IT".

80. Peter Asher, Linda Ronstadt's manager and producer, was part of a pop duet in 1960's called Peter and Gordon. What was the name of their UK no. 1 chart hit? A WORLD WITHOUT LOVE.

81. What did Linda Ronstadt say to Frank Sinatra during her concert when she noticed him sat in the audience? I HEAR YOU HAVE BEEN SINGING MY SONGS.

82. Why did Christopher Riddle leave his tuba at home when travelling to play in his father's orchestra for a motion picture Nelson was scoring for Warner Bros? There are two correct answers, either one will do but a bonus point if you get both. HE WANTED TO LEAVE SPACE IN THE PASSENGER SEAT FOR HIS GIRLFRIEND. HE WAS ADVISED THERE WERE NO PARTS IN THE SCORE FOR A TUBA.

83. Known as "The King of Bolero", with whom did Nelson record the single "Mexicali Rose"? LUCHO GATTICA.

84. *Yes............* was an album collaboration with Dinah Shore in 1958. Fill in the blank to complete the title. INDEED.

85. When Nelson put together the A-Z medley for Sinatra's *TV All Star Party* in 1983, Sinatra joined Vic Damone and Steve Lawrence for the final chorus of which song? ZING WENT THE STRINGS OF MY HEART.

86. Name the Nat "King" Cole tribute instrumental album Nelson recorded one year after Cole's death? NAT – AN ORCHESTRAL PORTRAIT OF NAT "KING" COLE.

87. What was the nickname Nelson gave to Screen Gems and when Christopher visited their offices? What was unusual about the chocolates they offered to guests? Half a point for each correct answer. SCREEN GERMS. THE CHOCOLATES WERE STAGE PROPS MADE OF RUBBER.

88. What was the type of music that Nelson used in his arrangement of the promo disc by film actress Yvonne De Carlo titled "Take it or Leave It"? GOOMBAY, A BAHAMIAN MUSIC GENRE.

89. What was the name of the producer who engaged Nelson's services for the TV series *Emergency* and *Project UFO*? JACK WEBB (AKA SGT. JOE FRIDAY IN DRAGNET).

90. Barbra Streisand asked that Paramount employ Nelson Riddle to be one of the orchestrators for *Funny Girl*. This was Streisand's film debut, and there were numerous rumours of unrest among other cast members who had their roles diminished at the behest of Streisand. What did director William Wyler reply when asked if working with Streisand had proved difficult? NOT AT ALL CONSIDERING IT WAS THE FIRST FILM SHE HAD DIRECTED.

91. Judy Garland visited the Riddle household and left something behind, what was it? PART OF A PLASTER CAST.

92. The film *Can Can* was released in 1960 and saw Nelson nominated for an Oscar once again. A famous Cole Porter song was left out of the film. What was the name of the song? Nelson compensated somewhat for the producer's omission; how did he achieve that? I LOVE PARIS. NELSON INCLUDED IT IN THE UNDERSCORE.

93. For the Sinatra album *Strangers in The Night,* Nelson used an instrument for the introduction in "Summer Wind" that hitherto had not been used to introduce a Sinatra song. What was the instrument used? AN ORGAN.

94. What would never end "Without a Song"? THE DAY WOULD NEVER END.

95. Nelson was involved with Stanley Kramer's film about Doctor T. How many fingers did the doctor have? FIVE THOUSAND.

96. Shirley Bassey combined with Nelson to record a number 5 hit in the early 60's. Later on in her career, this song was to become an important part of Bassey's live concerts. Name the song. WHAT NOW MY LOVE?

97. What time of day did Sinatra prefer to record and why? AT NIGHT AS HIS PIPES WERE LOOSER.

98. What song does Tony Christie describe as the best husband and wife song ever written? THE FOLKS WHO LIVE ON THE HILL.

99. In later years, Nelson felt his music was better appreciated in the UK and one other country than in his native USA. What was the other country? JAPAN.

100. Although very ill, Nelson travelled overnight from Los Angeles to perform his last gig with a 55-piece

orchestra at South Street Seaport in New York. This was an exhausting schedule but when asked by Christopher Riddle why he had committed to play in L.A only the night before, what was his reply? "I COULDN'T LET ELLA DOWN."

References:

AllMusic's reviews: *Songs for Swingin' Lovers and It's a Swingin' Affair.*

Ambient Exotica reviews*: Sea of Dreams* and *Love Tide.*

Oscar Peterson and Nelson Riddle album review*:* Andrew Cartmel *of London Jazz news.*

AllMusic's review: *There's Love and There's Love and There's Love* - Jason Ankeny

Frank Sinatra: An American Legend by Nancy Sinatra.

September in the Rain, by Peter Levinson.

All Star Party for Frank Sinatra: review by CBS.

Cross Country Suite review: Marc Myers.

Jonathan Schwartz interviews from 1983.

Sinatra, The Chairman James Kaplan.

The Man I Love review: William Ruhlmann.

Girl Singer, by Rosemary Clooney.

Simple Dreams, by Linda Ronstadt.

IMDb: *film trivia.*

I've Got You Under My Skin – Vanity Fair

ABOUT THE AUTHOR

Geoffrey Littlefield is a baby boomer born in London, England. His first foray into the entertainment world started at the age of thirteen when he appeared on BBC radio programme winning the prestigious Junior Sporting Chance trophy. The same year he had his first magazine article published having interviewed a number of Chelsea FC and England soccer players.

Alongside his encyclopaedic knowledge of sport, his love of music, especially The Great American Songbook, developed rapidly, resulting in Geoffrey moving into music management and record production. His written works continued and included an interview with American singer Vic Damone, described by Frank Sinatra as "having the best vocal equipment in the business. Geoffrey's acknowledged expertise and understanding of the songbook has generated several radio interviews and television presentations, both in the UK and USA.

Geoffrey continues to write, produce, and direct. Two movie projects as screenwriter are in development, together with the publication of a new book and documentary set for release later in 2021.

CHRISTOPHER RIDDLE

Christopher Riddle has contributed several first-hand accounts and memories to his father's biography. Christopher is the only one of Nelson's children to become a professional musician, he served his apprenticeship primarily as a bass trombonist in his father's orchestra, but also gained valuable experience with the orchestras of Buddy Rich, Henry Mancini, and Don Costa. He has backed many of the greatest singers of the 20th century including Frank Sinatra, Ella Fitzgerald, Sammy Davis Jr and Linda Ronstadt.

In addition to establishing himself as a renowned trombonist, Christopher became a veteran of the Hollywood recording studios. With the decline of his father's health, he became involved in all aspects of the band and ultimately became the leader of the Nelson Riddle orchestra (NRO).

Now in his later years this indefatigable performer finds time to compose and occasionally arrange and remains an ardent and committed advocate of preserving and promoting quality popular music for audiences world-wide.

For further information visit www.getmybook.tv

Index: